# The Boy from the Forest
Dr. Shay Efrat

D1527868

Producer & International Distributor
eBookPro Publishing
www.ebook-pro.com

**The Boy from the Forest**
**Dr. Shay Efrat**

Translation: Gilad Friedman

Contact: shaywp@gmail.com
ISBN 9798849085821

# THE BOY
# FROM THE
# FOREST

## THE HEART-WRENCHING WW2 TRUE STORY
## OF A HOLOCAUST SURVIVOR

## DR. SHAY EFRAT

*This book is dedicated to the memory of my beloved late grandfather, **Moshe Efrat**, who instilled in me the importance of Holocaust remembrance and genuine family values, and who always showed his true love for me.*

# ACKNOWLEDGEMENTS

I am eternally grateful to the members of the Sucha-Lahav family who gave their blessing to this project and courageously opened their hearts to me. Without them, this book would never have been written.

I wish to thank my beloved wife Molly; my children Gal, Lilach, and Tomer; my mother Shula and my father Hillel – all of whom, in their own special way, assisted me greatly in the writing of this book.

# CONTENTS

# FOREWORD BY PROF. GIDEON GREIF

The detailed testimony of Holocaust survivor Shmuel Sucha and the stories of his family members are the product of in-depth interviews conducted with them by Dr. Shai Efrat. This testimony transcends the personal world of Shmuel Sucha, a Holocaust survivor.

"The Final Solution to the Jewish Question" dictated that all Jews be put to death; thus, despite the personal tones of each and every survivor's story, a Holocaust survivor represents not only himself – but Jewry as a whole.

In this sense, the story of Shmuel Sucha is the story of the Holocaust – the greatest catastrophe ever to befall the Jewish People.

It is a story of resistance and heroism, of restoration and rebuilding, of the founding of a new generation. It is a story which is relevant to all Jews, wherever they may be. Sucha's personal story affords us a closer look at the mysterious, sensitive and complex issue of the Holocaust.

One of the more striking features of this book is the impressive and moving manner in which Dr. Efrat elicits the testimony from Shmuel and his family members. He steers them toward unconventional and diverse themes which all survivors must face up to, reflect on, and address.

Dr. Efrat masterfully conducts his interviews, providing a complex, diverse, and original perspective for the reader, as well as a thought-provoking struggle with issues such as morals and ethics during desperate times; collective and personal responsibility; patterns of human behavior during extreme distress; solidarity; retribution; relations with the Germans and their children; and many other issues which hold great importance for us and for future generations.

What makes this book so unique is the intricate network of layers embedded and intertwined in it – life, destiny, regeneration, reaction, the Jewish struggle.

At the same time, this uniquely complex Jewish story of one Holocaust survivor involves other inseparable parts which make up the whole: these are the lives of his wife, his children, and his acquaintances. Thus Dr. Efrat offers us a more complex, sophisticated and profound outlook on the Holocaust, the life of a survivor and the lives of those other survivors he represents.

Dr. Efrat also shines a bright light on various secondary spheres relating to the Holocaust: life in Jewish towns; the escape to the forests; the fight of the Partisans; the betrayal of the Jews by their non-Jewish neighbors; and most obviously, the fascinating and complicated life of a survivor post-Holocaust – on the road to rehabilitation, regeneration and revival in the historic Promised Land.

Dr. Efrat, with the generous help of Shmuel's story, paints a colorful picture of the classic Jewish *shtetl* in Volyn Oblast (formerly the Polish region of Volyn). Once a vibrant area teeming with Jewish life, a world of color, craft, and creation, the region was brutally obliterated by the Germans during the Holocaust.

This may be the Holocaust story of one survivor and his hometown of Bereźne, but in many ways, it is a story which happened over and over again in Volyn and indeed throughout eastern Europe. In this aspect, it is a fully representative story.

Dr. Efrat's method is that of the personal interview, an oral documentation of history. Historians have long debated the authenticity and historical merit of this form of documentation, and were infamously reluctant to appreciate it; much greater importance had been placed on written documentation.

Nowadays, however, it is no longer a matter of doubt that where the Holocaust is concerned, one cannot outline the history of this period without taking into account the testimonies of its survivors. These testimonies began to pile up at a rate of knots even as early as the end of the Holocaust itself.

Without addressing these testimonies, one cannot begin to comprehend the feelings of those Jews; their reactions and understanding of the world around them; their daily heroic struggle and survival; and most of all, their bottomless suffering.

These aspects of the story might never have been brought to our attention absent the oral history. Moreover, these aspects have almost never been recorded in any official document, with the stark exception of personal journals kept by Jews in the Holocaust. It is this fact that highlights the colossal importance of oral testimonies. They are unreservedly vital to studying the Holocaust, and are an absolute necessity if one wishes to understand and analyze it.

This book is an indispensable work which uniquely contributes to the understanding of complex moral and ethical dilemmas facing the Jews during the Holocaust, as well as the choices they made in order to survive, to fight, to live another day – thereby thwarting the Germans' nefarious scheme of obliterating the Jewish people from the face of the earth.

# PREFACE BY THE AUTHOR

Shmuel Sucha and myself both live in the northern Israeli kibbutz of Shamir. My earliest significant memory of Shmuel is from the mid-1970s, when I was about 10 years old.

Like most children my age in the kibbutz, I used to visit the petting zoo several times a week. Among the various animals there were goats, sheep, chickens and rabbits; we learned to care for them and look after them.

My love of animals and the petting zoo were in part due to the caretaker who worked there at the time, and greeted us every morning upon our arrival. His name was Shmuel Sucha, or "Shmulik", as we affectionately called him. My foremost memory of Shmulik is of an energetic and affable man who was constantly on the move, always scurrying amongst the pens and cages. We children were much younger, but it was us who were always following him, trying to keep up the pace.

At the time, I didn't know the first thing about Shmuel's personal life, certainly not his past in the Holocaust – in those days he rarely ever wrote about it or spoke of it in public.

My second significant memory of Shmuel is from 1983. I was a senior at *Einot Yarden* High School, and volunteered to organize the annual Holocaust memorial ceremony at the school.

I say volunteered – rather than being selected or appointed – because the topic of the Holocaust had already intrigued me as a teenager. It was only natural for me to volunteer; more accurately, I felt a *need* to do it. I never gave it much thought as a teenager, but being a third-generation survivor of the Holocaust from Romania and Poland – along with the stories I had heard, primarily from my late grandfather Moshe Efrat – must have left a deep impression on me.

Having heard parts of his personal story, and knowing he wrote poems about the Holocaust, I invited Shmuel to participate in the ceremony.

Shmuel eagerly accepted the invitation. Students and teachers alike were riveted by his storytelling. There were two things he said which I found deeply impactful. Gesturing out the window at a bright blue sky and trees in full bloom, he said: "What you need to understand is that even on beautiful days such as this one, Jews were put to death in their thousands."

The second thing he said was loaded with vivid imagery, as is his custom: "The Jews were used to handling bad times like reeds in the wind: bowing their heads and waiting for the storm to pass… they tried to do the same in the Holocaust, but this was different. They were caught unawares and perished."

In 2001, as a drama therapy student, I took a course titled "A Living Bridge", dealing with mental fortitude, capacity for survival, and recovery from trauma. One of the tasks in the course was to interview someone who had experienced, overcome, and survived hardships in his or her life. Immediately I knew that I would be interviewing Shmuel Sucha. Along with two fellow students, Yael and Ronen, we met with Shmuel and conducted the interview. I distinctly remember how deeply impressed my colleagues were with Shmuel and his fascinating story.

In 2013, I began studying for a doctorate in psychology. After much deliberation over the topic of my thesis, I elected to cover the moral dilemmas that many Jews faced both during and after the Holocaust. I studied the views of teenagers on the manner in which the Jews faced these dilemmas. I gradually began to feel a strong urge to revisit Shmuel's story, to hear it once more – and this time, to properly document it. My reasons for doing so were threefold: Firstly, and most simply put, I was curious to learn more. Secondly, I innately understood that memorializing his story while he was still alive was of the utmost importance. Thirdly – and this was an aspiration that at the time was still somewhat vague – I wished to write a book about Shmuel and the Holocaust, and thus tackle the Holocaust "hands-on" by focusing on an actual survivor.

In February 2016, while in the midst of my studies, I began to interview Shmuel at his home in Shamir. Most of these interviews – conducted on-and-off until July 2020 – were recorded; some were videotaped. All told, I interviewed him twenty times for a total of around sixty hours. Shmuel recounted impressively detailed stories of his survival during the Holocaust and of his life in the years following. Each interview resulted in more questions to be tackled at the next. It was a highly engrossing, potentially endless process, as at every turn Shmuel's riveting answers raised even more compelling questions. Alas, for these interviews to result in a finished product, we had to stop at some point.

Those absorbing sessions resulted in incredibly broad and comprehensive information, coupled with prodigious attention to detail with regards to content, thoughts, and feelings. An additional beneficial by-product was how close we both became. Shmuel is a charming, kind-hearted, and intelligent man who possesses a highly developed and unique sense of humor. On occasion – and this always brings a smile to my face – he refers to himself in the third person, calling himself "Shmil" or "Shmilik".

Shmuel's method of recounting the story of the Holocaust is tantalizingly unique. It fuses extreme pain with savvy humor, and perhaps surprisingly, he often prompts his audience to smile or laugh. In my view this does nothing to desecrate the memory of the Holocaust. On the contrary – it helps one to understand and empathize with the pain. After all, laughter and humor are, first and foremost, useful defense mechanisms against hardship, casting a positive light on what can often be a difficult life. Whenever Shmuel tells an entertaining story – or for that matter, chooses to tackle a heavy topic with his unique brand of humor – he chuckles and winks, making his audience more comfortable and more receptive to the story. Despite never officially receiving a higher education (as he proudly admits himself), Shmuel is self-taught and possesses an admirably eclectic general knowledge. Among his interests are the history of the Holocaust and World War II, literature, poetry, and much more.

The decision to expand the story beyond Shmuel's personal life to the story of his family arose naturally during the interviews. This was due to my desire to delve deeper into the effects and implications of the Holocaust on a personal, familial, and multi-generational level. Thankfully, his family accepted my request – and thus a second part of the book was born.

In October of 2019, I visited western Ukraine with my wife Molly. As part of the trip, we visited the region of Volyn, including Shmuel's hometown of Bereźne. It was a deeply moving and fascinating excursion which gave me much perspective on life. We walked through the streets of Bereźne, saw the death pits at the edge of the town, and visited the villages and forests that Shmuel had described in his story. We also traveled to the village of Kurhany, where Shmuel stayed for a few months prior to the killing of the Jews of Bereźne (and was thus saved from the fate of his townspeople). At the edge of the village we happened upon a young boy, who was approximately the age Shmuel had been in the summer of 1942, around the time he had stayed at Kurhany. Imagining Shmuel at the same spot made me realize the terror and helplessness he must have felt upon being banished by the farmer he had stayed with to fend for himself.

Life is one great mystery. I had never planned on writing about Shmuel or the Holocaust, but the paths I took have led me to publish this book, and for that I am grateful.

# HISTORICAL BACKGROUND: BEREŹNE AND VOLYN DURING THE HOLOCAUST

The western Ukrainian town of Bereźne, on the banks of the Sluch River, is situated about 40 miles northeast of Rivne, the capital of the Volyn region. Formerly in Poland, the entire area is today a part of Ukraine.

Between the two world wars, from 1918 to 1939, some 250,000 Jews lived in Volyn, which was part of eastern Poland (an area the Jews called "Galicia"). Most of the villages and towns of Volyn – Bereźne included – had a large Jewish population, often even a majority. In September of 1939, Nazi Germany and the USSR partitioned Poland between them in accordance with the Molotov-Ribbentrop Pact.

The pact was signed in Moscow on 23 August 1939 by German Foreign Minister Joachim von Ribbentrop and Soviet Foreign Minister Vyacheslav Molotov, and ultimately became one of the chief causes of the second world war. The agreement covered two main items: a non-aggression pact, and the partitioning of Poland between the two nations. In September of 1939, western Poland was annexed by Germany, while eastern Poland – Volyn included – was annexed by the Soviet Union. The river Bug, in total around 500 miles in length, acted as the border between the two nations. The pact was violated on 22 June 1941 with the German invasion of the Soviet Union, dubbed "Operation Barbarossa".

Between the end of June and the beginning of July of 1941, as part of Barbarossa, the Germans occupied the region of Volyn. It was later liberated by the Soviet Red Army in early 1944. Since then the area has been a part of Ukraine – at first Soviet Ukraine, and since 1991 it has been a part of independent Ukraine.

At the time World War II broke out in September 1939, the majority of Bereźne's some 3,500 Jews were religious, and most were traders or craftsmen. They constituted a large majority of the town's population, alongside Ukrainians, Poles, Germans, and a small Gypsy community. The town was known for its vibrant Jewish cultural life – including synagogues, Jewish day schools, cultural centers, Zionist youth movements, etc. (Bigil, 1954; Sucha, 2001; Spector, 1990).

On July 6, 1941, the Bereźne area was captured by the German 6th Army (a part of Army Group South). Immediately upon the town's capture, the local Ukrainians looted Jewish possessions and brutally beat them with impunity. A short while after the occupation, local Jews were forced to wear a special distinguishing mark – a white armband with a blue Star of David, which was later replaced by the yellow "Jewish Badge". They were subjected to forced labor in the peat mines and at the paper factory in the nearby town of Mokvyn. Approximately 300 young Jews were sent to a labor camp in the city of Kostopil', 20 miles southwest of Bereźne.

On 6 October 1941, the Germans enclosed 3,000 of Bereźne's Jews in a well-guarded, sealed-off ghetto. Another neighboring ghetto was built in the vicinity, where several hundred Jews who were traders or professionals had been living with their families. Upon their relocation to the ghetto, almost all of the

Jews' possessions were confiscated by the Germans. Both ghettos suffered from severe overcrowding; there were anywhere from 10 to 20 people living in each room. Each Jew who worked for the Germans received a ration of 150 or 200 grams of bread per day, along with a portion of diluted soup. Rations for Jews who did not work were limited to a mere 100 grams of bread per day. Naturally, this caused widespread hunger in the ghetto. Worse, the cold weather, overcrowding, disease, and forced labor resulted in much sickness and death. Many of the ghetto's inhabitants died during the winter of 1941-1942.

Similar conditions – including harsh decrees, forced labor, and overcrowded ghettos – existed in all places where Jews were present in Volyn. However, in some places, the mass murder of Jews took place even before there had been time to place them in ghettos.

From June 1941 to July 1942, mass murder of Jews took place by firing squad into pre-dug pits throughout the region of Volyn. The killings were carried out by *Einsatzkommando* 4a, a sub-group of *Einsatzgruppe* C – one of the SS death squads which specialized in murdering Jews (the SS being the major paramilitary organization under Nazi rule). The German police, along with Polish and Ukrainian militias who collaborated with the Nazis, all took part in the murders; the *Wehrmacht* (the German military) provided logistical support for the killing squads. During the first year of Nazi occupation, some 20% of Volyn's Jews were murdered. The comprehensive killing spree perpetrated against the Jews of western Poland began in July 1942, and eventually arrived in Bereźne as well.

The fate that befell the Jews of eastern Poland, while no less gruesome, was somewhat different to that of the Jews of western Poland. In the west, the vast majority of the Jews were executed in the gas chambers of the six extermination camps established in Poland: Treblinka, Majdanek, Belzec, Sobibor, Chelmno and Auschwitz-Birkenau. In the east, however, the Jews were executed by shooting into pre-dug pits. While the killings were carried out by the aforementioned German killing squads, they were happily aided by local Polish and Ukrainian militias, made up of locals motivated by antisemitic sentiment. Moreover, motivated by nationalist sentiment, they assisted the Germans in their war against the Soviets; they viewed the Russians as occupiers and despised them no less than they did the Jews.

The Bereźne ghetto, much like in other Jewish towns, was autonomously run by the *Judenrat*, a local Jewish council which presided over the Jews at the Germans' behest. Among other duties, the Judenrat ran a public kitchen which provided the locals with the ever-insufficient rations of food. According to the ghetto's survivors, the head of the Judenrat, Yoel Gilber, was a weak man; the ghetto was de facto ruled by two other Judenrat members, aided by Meyer Keiler (Kremnitsky), the head of the Jewish Police. According to testimony, these men abused the ghetto's inhabitants, stole their possessions, and extorted money from them. Following the eradication of the ghetto, Keiler fled to the forests and joined Medvedev's Partisan brigade. However, Jewish partisans from Bereźne demanded he be tried for his actions. He was sentenced to death and subsequently executed.

Under the command of local SS commander *Oberscharführer* (senior squad leader) Alfred Klanz, the Bereźne ghetto was overseen mainly by a few German policemen and local Ukrainian collaborators enlisted by the Germans. The Jewish Police also played a very active role in the supervision of the ghetto. In mid-June 1942, in preparation for the planned mass killings, more Jews were transferred to Bereźne from the neighboring villages, among them – Mokovyn, Malynsk, Yarynivka, Orlivka, Polyany and others. Subsequently, the number of Jews imprisoned in the ghetto rose to around 4,000.

Between July and October of 1942, the Germans carried out the final phase of the extermination of the Jews of Volyn. The killings were overseen by the SS and carried out by German policemen along with local Ukrainian militias. The method, as usual in these areas, was by firing squad into pre-dug death pits. The German army provided logistical support and security for the killings.

On 25 August 1942, the Bereźne ghetto was surrounded by German policemen and their local collaborators. They led the Jews to three large pits near the town cemetery, dug in advance by local Ukrainians. The perpetrators proceeded to murder all of the Jews – men, women and children. While the first group of victims lay at the bottom of the pit, the next group was forced to lie on top of them, and were also subsequently shot. Upon completion of the killings, the pits were covered with dirt. The massacre lasted two days, as the murderers were not able to complete their task within one day.

Prior to the killings (dubbed "Aktion" by the Germans), the Jews were warned about their imminent demise by Rosenfeld, one of the local German commanders, and by Marchuk, the Ukrainian foreman of the peat mines. Some 200 Jews managed to escape and sought shelter, but most of them were ultimately apprehended or turned in by locals, and were also murdered. The remaining Jews did not even attempt to flee. Russian officials pegged the number of Jews murdered during those two days at 3,680.

Several Jews who escaped the ghetto – along with those who had hidden in the area prior to the massacre, and those who had escaped the Kostopil' labor camp – sought shelter in the forests around Bereźne. On rare occasions, they were given shelter and were placed in hiding by locals who became known as Righteous Gentiles. Those hiding in the forests gradually and spontaneously organized into groups, facing daily life-threatening dangers of hunger, cold, and local collaborators who would attempt to hunt them down and hand them over to the Germans (or murder them directly). There was also a minority of locals who assisted the Jews, mainly with food. A small minority of the Jews later joined the Soviet partisans in the area. There was a small group of Jews who had fled the Bereźne massacre and formed a fighter group aimed at exacting retribution against Ukrainian collaborators, sabotaging the Rivne-Sarny rail line, and protecting those Jews who joined the group. They linked up with Colonel Medvedev's Russian partisan brigade and headquartered close by, near the village of Rudnia-Bobrowska. It was in this brigade that Yosef Golov of Bereźne served as deputy commander of the patrol unit, and several other members of the Jewish group joined the brigade. The others fled north toward southern Byelorussia, in search of areas free of the German invaders. While crossing the Sarny-Olevs'k rail line, they encountered a German unit. Some were killed while others fled, and the group dispersed. Several days later, some of the survivors joined the partisan unit of Moshe Gildenman nicknamed "Dyadya Misha".

In January of 1944 the Bereźne area was liberated by the Red Army. Bereźne itself was liberated on January 10. Following the capture of the area by the Soviets, the Jews who had survived and remained in hiding – whether in the forests or in the homes of Righteous Gentiles – were free to emerge from hiding. It is estimated that of the 3,500 Jews living in Bereźne prior to the Nazi invasion, only around 150 survived (Bigil, 1954; Breier, 1996; Finkelstein, 1994; Spector, 1990; Digital archive of Yad Vashem, 2017).

# PART I

## SHMUEL SUCHA
## I SURVIVED TO TELL MY STORY

I'm an old Jew by now.

I'm eighty-nine years old, but the Holocaust is something I relive every single day.

Telling my story means so much to me, because it is a way for the memory of what happened there to live on. It is a living tribute to my murdered family.

The greatest danger is forgetting. The worst death is the death of memory.

And so, by passing on these stories from generation to generation, the memories will remain intact.

This is why my greatest desire in life is to tell my stories and pass on these memories.

It is also my own way to never forget: by telling these stories, I recall them again and again.

The Polish poet Zbigniew Herbert once said: "And if the city falls but a single man escapes, He will carry the city within himself."

I carry my Holocaust memories within myself, and pass them on.

**I survived to tell my story** – that is my own destiny.

I am always willing to tell my Holocaust story.

Whenever I tell it, the words flow like a river – unbridled, unchecked.

I tell the story as it happened – no frills, no embellishments. I have no interest in distorting reality, nor in sugar-coating it, as many other Holocaust survivors sometimes tend to do... my memory serves me well, and I tell my stories exactly as they happened.

I am not ashamed of anything I have done. Other survivors feel they've acted unethically, immorally even. But not me. The Holocaust is ingrained in me so deeply, I relive it every single day. In fact, the older I get, the more I think about it.

I find myself thinking endlessly of my sister, my mother; all the members of my family who were brutally murdered. It may be they who are dead, but it is I who feel like I am put to death every day, over and over.

I think of how they died, and try to imagine what it would be like if I had been there with them that day.

In a way I feel sorry that I didn't die along with everyone else – the pain and guilt I feel for having survived while they did not, is a burden that has always weighed down on me.

And yet – not all is dark and bleak. I can appreciate and enjoy life. I enjoy eating good food, and I have a sense of humor. Occasionally I'll even write a funny story and chuckle to myself. On the inside, however, the laughter is always tinged with sadness.

I try to keep fit; I make sure to walk 2 miles on my treadmill every day. I doubt there are many people my age who could manage that!

Walking feels natural to me. Not walking just feels wrong, as if something in my brain is off balance. It's as if I'm collecting rust. And then when I walk again, I feel like I'm shedding all that rust.

The mind is like a riverbed. Devoid of water, it begins to decay. Each person has his own riverbed, but many of them are decaying. If your riverbed is full of water, you will find your way.

It's these metaphors which help me to think and keep my brain active. Ever since I was a boy, I've always used metaphors. I remember how proud my parents were of me for being smart enough to be able to use them to express myself.

My story and the story of the Holocaust are inextricably linked.

In my mind, the Holocaust is like an ocean of blood, and I am but one drop in that ocean.

I'm not sure anyone can accurately describe the experience of the Holocaust.

Recounting even one day of that horrific reality seems like an impossible task. The Holocaust was, as we call it, "outside the boundaries of life".

A Jew was considered less than human, and could be murdered at any moment.

We need to study and learn and tell the story of the Holocaust, most importantly because it is so difficult to comprehend and yet so easy to forget. Humans tend to want to forget the terrible things.

And yet – if this horrific chapter of history is forgotten, men will not be afraid to do evil.

Just as it happened decades ago, when "ordinary men" brought about the evils of the Holocaust.

# CHAPTER 1:
# CHILDHOOD MEMORIES

I was born in a small town named Bereźne in the region of Volyn. Up until 1939, the area was part of Poland, but it has been a part of Ukraine since 1945, when the Russians annexed east Poland to Soviet Ukraine at the end of World War II. After Ukraine became an independent country in 1990, Volyn became a part of western Ukraine.

Generally speaking, the Russians engaged in quite a bit of population transfer and border shifting, both prior to the war and after it. My hometown's 3,500 Jews were a large majority – there were only 500 or so non-Jews living there at the time, including Ukrainians, Poles, and Gypsies. There were several smaller Ukrainian and Polish villages surrounding Bereźne; there were a few Jews who lived there as well. Up until 1939, there was also a sizable German population, but following the Russian occupation of east Poland in September 1939 (as part of the Molotov-Ribbentrop Pact between the Russians and the Germans), the Germans mostly relocated to Germany. To populate the now-empty German villages, the Russians brought in Ukrainian inhabitants from the areas they had occupied in eastern Poland.

Prior to the Holocaust, the region of Volyn was home to around a quarter of a million Jews. Many famous rabbis lived there, as well as authors such as Haim Nahman Bialik. Famous

Israeli author and broadcaster Dan Ben Amotz was also born in Rivne, not far from Bereźne. I recall the excitement and hubbub when Zionist leader Ze'ev Jabotinsky gave a speech in our town. My father, an avid Zionist, was especially enthusiastic. I still remember the little yellow donation box we kept at home in which we used to put money to contribute to the Zionist cause.

Bereźne is situated in the sprawling farming plains of western Ukraine. The area is well known for growing grain crops such as wheat and barley, as well as for its cattle, sheep, and horses. As children we used to wade in the Sluch River which winds through the town.

The name of the town derives from "Bereza", which is Russian for a birch tree. The birch is a tall, lofty, beautiful tree, with a white bark and lush, rich green foliage. If you cut the bark, you can drink the sap which is colorless and sweet. I remember the townspeople bringing a large tin vessel to the base of the trees, cutting the bark and extracting the sap for a cool, refreshing drink. Birch forests are abundant around Bereźne, and indeed throughout Volyn. These forests played a major role in our ability to survive during the war – without them, we would have had nowhere to hide.

When we hid from the Ukrainians and the Germans during the war, we used to drink the birch sap and it helped us to survive. Unfortunately, the juice was only extractable during the spring. I was once told that there is a potent fungus that grows on the birch, which is ground to a fine powder and used to cure all sorts of diseases. The Ukrainians used the tree's branches to make broomsticks. When burned, the birch's ashes are also used to make laundry soap. When I lived in hiding in the woods, we used the ashes to wash with: when it rained, we'd rub the ashes mixed with rainwater on our bodies and it would create the effect of soap bubbles.

I was born in 1930 or 1931. I'm not quite sure when because in my town, as far as I can recall, no one celebrated birthdays. In fact, it was only when I was about sixteen and I enlisted in the Palmach (the elite fighting force of the Haganah, the Jewish underground army during the British Mandate of Palestine) that I was actually required to determine my age. The name "Palmach" is a Hebrew acronym for "P'lugot Makhatz", loosely translated as "strike force".

And so, upon being required to determine my age, I chose my year of birth as 1931, and June as my birth month – so that I could celebrate my birthday in the summer. There are precious few people who get to choose their own birthday... my choice meant that I was 11 years old when the Jews of Bereźne were murdered in August of 1942.

As a small boy I used to study Torah in a "Cheider" – a Hebrew study class for pre-school boys. The teacher was usually the rabbi. This was before the war, and the area was controlled by Poland. I was about four or five years old, and I didn't want to go to class. My father, Natan, would spank me, drape me over his shoulder, and force me to go to Cheider.

There was one boy – his name escapes me – who used to cry because he couldn't pronounce the letter "B". He used to say "Rerre" instead of "Rebbe". The rabbi would spank him with a stick to get him to learn and stop crying. The rabbi's name was Moshe Miriam. He would eat throughout the lesson and spank anyone who didn't study hard enough or who had the tenacity to interrupt.

We used to study the Bible. I vaguely remember random stories about Jacob and Sisera… there's still a part of me that remembers those things. Later on I went to a Jewish religious day school. There was another Jewish elementary school in the town which was not as religious. The area's high school, which was not Jewish, was situated in Rivne, the largest city in the region. Most Jewish children did not go there, but rather stayed in the town and joined their parents at work.

There are a lot of things that I don't really remember… it's pretty much a blur. I grew up in a reasonably well-off family, even if we weren't rich. My father's last name was "Sucha", which means "Plough" in Polish. After the Holocaust, when I went to the youth movement, I remember making an embarrassing mistake when they asked me to spell my name. I wrote "Suka" instead of Sucha. The problem was that in Russian, "Suka" means "bitch". I did get laughed at about it for quite a while… in any case, my mother's family had lived in Rivne, the main city of Volyn, for many generations. My father's family came from Bereźne. My maternal grandmother's name was Beila. Grandma Beila had a stall at the Bereźne market, and she used to sell seeds, candy, and soda to the farmers who used to come and sell their wares at the market. She always used to put a bit of extra weight on the scales. There was a saying amongst the Jews at the time, "it is obligatory to cheat the *goyim* (gentiles)." I saw her do it with my own eyes. My mother's name was Yenta, and she used to help out at the market. She was also the one who raised us and basically ran the household. My father's name was Natan Sucha (my eldest son is named after him). His father's name was Srulke (Israel), but his nickname was "Srulke der Deutsch" ("German Srulke"), because he used to trade with the German villagers who lived in the area. When my father joined him in the trade business, he was given the nickname "Nusskin der Deutsch". They traded mostly horses and cows. Who knows, perhaps if the Holocaust hadn't happened, I would have become a trader too… they could have named me "Shmilke der Deutsch".

On occasion I would join my father on his business trips to Rivne, on his way to buy salt. On one of our trips there, while traveling through one of the villages, I was bitten by a dog who had escaped his leash. I still have the scars to prove it! Of course I had no way of knowing it at the time, but my intimate knowledge of the area thanks to those trips with my father ultimately proved essential to my survival whilst hiding in the woods during the Holocaust.

My younger sister's name was Batya, named after my maternal grandmother, but she was always called "Buzha", which means "Beautiful". My grandmother's last name was Fischman. Old man Fischman, my paternal grandfather (whose first name I can't remember), went to Canada in the 1930s and stayed there. The original plan was for his wife and daughter to move there with him once he had settled in, but unfortunately they lost contact. This was a recurring theme amongst many eastern European Jewish families.

Ours was never considered a family of intellectuals. The one person who was noticeably intelligent was my mother, Yenta. She had graduated from high school, no mean feat for a Jewish woman at the time. She was originally from the village of Mezhyrich, not far from Bereźne. She came from a family of engineers and intellectuals, some of whom lived in Rivne, which also had a university. My mother had two uncles who lived in Rivne – Israel Fischman, a water pump engineer, and Leiker Fischman. Not one of her family members survived the Holocaust.

As was customary at the time, my parents' marriage was arranged. They were married in Rivne, but lived in Bereźne right from the start. My father ate pork, and my mother – who was observant – used to chide him: "Nusskin, you'll burn in hell!" Like my father, I too eat pork. I get it at the convenience store in the kibbutz and eat it whenever I want to. But my father kept the pork in a little alcove in the wall, because my mother wouldn't let him keep it in the pantry. He also had an affinity for vodka. He had served in the Polish army, and knew how to fire a rifle. Despite his vices, he still frequented the synagogue. That was our home – not devout by any means, but a Jewish home nonetheless.

I was a mischievous boy, quick on my feet, and I used to get in quite a bit of trouble. I remember picking apples from the public park's trees and eating them. I remember the first time my mother sent me to fetch water from the well. I was quite small, and the bucket was heavy and all the water spilled on the way home. But I didn't despair – I went right back to the well and got more water. This time I was more careful and I made it home with most of the water. My mother hugged me and said "Shmilik, you're a big boy now!" She used the nickname "Shmilik" when she referred to me, and that's the name I occasionally use for myself to this day.

At home we spoke Yiddish, because that was the fundamental language of Diaspora Jews. All Jewish people in Poland and eastern Europe spoke Yiddish; it was taught in kindergartens, schools and Cheiders. During the interwar period (from 1918 to 1939) the Poles ruled Volyn and eastern Poland, and the official language was Polish. So I speak some Yiddish and some Polish, most of which I've forgotten. I speak Russian better, because when the Russians occupied eastern Poland in September 1939, Russian became the official language. As a teenager in Bereźne after the war, I went to a Russian school and the townspeople spoke Russian. While we didn't speak Hebrew, we did know how to read Hebrew from the prayer books and the Bible. It was the Bible that helped Diaspora Jews to maintain their tradition and identity for two thousand years. It served as a homeland for people with no land to call home. The Jewish nation is the oldest living nation. It is a source of great pride to be Jewish! The Jews learned written Hebrew because they prayed in Hebrew and their holy books are mostly in Hebrew. The language warmed the hearts of Jews like a furnace warms one in the winter. In the Diaspora it was known as "The Holy Tongue", and leading rabbis knew how to speak it as well. The Jews were by and large successful intellectuals, which caused great envy among the gentiles.

In September of 1939 the Russians occupied eastern Poland, which I remember clearly. The Jews hadn't suffered much under Polish rule, but once the Russians came they felt that the wind had changed and were slightly more wary. Among the Russian military there were many Jewish officers, which was a source of some comfort. Russia had about three million Jews, and many of them were officers and soldiers in the Russian Red Army. We asked the Russians how life was in Russia, and they replied:

"Like God in Odessa". It's a Russian saying meaning "all is good and well". The Russians also sent communist officials to run the town. Some of them just pretended to be communist. Every aspect of life was run by the Soviets – schools, trades and more. The Russians sent over teachers to instill the communist spirit in the locals.

I would say that on balance, our lives changed for the better once the Russians came. My father who had been a cattle trader, now worked for the Russians. As part of the Molotov-Ribbentrop Pact, the Russians had committed to supply the Germans with meat, and my father was in charge of transporting cows by train from Volyn to Kyiv, the Ukrainian capital. He would sell the cows there and bring back various items, mostly shoes and clothes. There was one time where he brought back a pair of ice skates for me. The town's Jews used to send their relatives letters in Kyiv with my father. Things were better then, but not for long.

# CHAPTER 2:
# UNDER A CLOUD OF DANGER

On June 22, 1941, the Germans invaded the Soviet Union. I remember waking up to loud noises in the middle of the night. German planes flew over the town, and the Russian army was mobilized in the area. In the morning we saw Russian infantry units heading west toward Poland. The soldiers marched in faded khaki uniforms with ten-bullet magazines in their semi-automatic rifles. Less than a week later, they had returned. They looked bad; they seemed exhausted and frightened. Those who passed through the town were given water. One Russian soldier gave me a fountain pen. My father was extremely concerned and asked the soldiers, "So what's going to happen?" The Russian raised his rifle in response and said, "Come take up arms and join the fight."

The Russian army retreated hastily eastward, and the Germans pursued them almost all the way back to Moscow. For every town and village, the arrival of the Germans meant a death sentence for the Jews. Of course, the Jews weren't aware of this yet. If they had had any inkling of what the Germans were about to do, they would have joined the Russians on their eastward retreat, and perhaps half of them would have been saved… but of course it never occurred to them and they stayed put.

I was a very nimble young boy. Today I am a fraction as sprightly as I used to be. I guess that's what kept me alive, because

I was so close to death on multiple occasions. There was a time where I believed I was invincible, that I was immortal, that God had chosen me to live forever and tell the story of the Holocaust. There was a Polish poet named Zbigniew Herbert who wrote: You were saved not in order to live; you have little time; you must give testimony! That is my motto which I borrowed from him. German philosopher Ferdinand Lasalle once said, "Aussprechen was ist!" (Get it all out) - that is another motto of mine. I lived in order to tell the story and get everything out. The concept of testifying to the horrors of what had happened, had been lodged in my mind ever since I left the forest upon the area's liberation, but it was dormant for quite a while until it was finally realized. Vague though it was at the time, it most certainly was an inherent part of my personality. I think what I mean to say is that I had always wanted to tell my story – but I never felt like it was the right thing to do, philosophically or emotionally speaking.

I wasn't the only one with those thoughts. It was the prevailing sentiment among the Jews who had survived. They spoke of the importance of telling the story to the world, but they also wished desperately to rebuild their lives. The lucky few who had any family left were split amongst those who wished to go back to their old lives, and those who wished to get out of there as soon as possible – whether to the Holy Land or elsewhere. Those who had lost their families, especially the younger ones, wished to rebuild a new family. Once survival is no longer first and foremost day in and day out, one begins to contemplate this sort of thing quite seriously.

The Germans didn't murder the Jews in our town right away, as they had done in other parts of the Soviet Union. Each area had a "regional commander", a German officer in charge of the Jews in his region – and later, entrusted with their executions. The Jews were like sheep – before you kill them, you shear them. The German commanders liked to extract as much as they could out of the Jews before killing them. They took their possessions, wore them down, and once they were penniless and weak – they would kill them. The Germans built an empire using these methods. They took whatever they wanted – radios, bicycles – if you had it, they would take it. I still remember my Uncle Meyer's bicycle. Sometimes he would let me ride with him – I can still hear his panting as he exerted all that effort. The Germans confiscated all the bicycles they could get their hands on and gave them to Ukrainian policemen. They took everything, even before they put the Jews in the ghetto. At that point, the Germans weren't even that bad. We children used to do odd jobs for them in return for food. Sometimes even for free, just because we were afraid to refuse. I remember cleaning a Wehrmacht soldier's bicycle for him and got my finger caught in the chain. My finger is still crooked to this day! The German soldier bandaged my wound and gave me a piece of candy. My mother, who knew German, thanked him and told him he was a good man. His chilling reply was, "Just you wait, lady. Soon the SS will be here and then you'll see." But she didn't believe him.

The SS was the special paramilitary unit of the Nazi regime. They were an independent army and did not answer to the Wehrmacht – the more "conventional" German military. They were the ones in charge of murdering the Jews, although the Wehrmacht soldiers and police certainly played their part as well. There was one time when my father took a shipment of cows to the train station to send them to Germany and was lucky to even get back alive after being shot at. The Germans would occasionally take potshots at the Jews transporting cattle just for fun… a Jewish life was worthless to them, and the Germans and the Ukrainians too, could kill any Jew they saw whenever they pleased.

I remember once I saw a German military vehicle stop by an elderly Jew walking down the street. Three Wehrmacht soldiers disembarked, looking cheerful. One of them called out to the old man, "Stop, come here!" The Jew had no choice and he walked over to them, removing his hat as all Jews were required to do when they encountered Germans. One of them pulled out a pair of scissors and just cut off half of the man's beard! They then got into the car and drove off. They weren't looking to kill anyone; they were just having a bit of fun humiliating an old Jew. It was their sick little twisted game, perhaps a way of passing the time - they knew they could do the Jews whatever they pleased.

There was another incident when I happened to be at my Aunt Chaike's house, when suddenly two German Wehrmacht soldiers showed up at the doorstep. They were there to confiscate clothes for the army. This was by no means an isolated incident – German soldiers would take belongings and food from the Jews all the time. Even the local Ukrainians weren't immune to this. Aunt Chaike held her little boy and said, "We are poor people." One of the Germans replied, "You aren't people, you're Jews." This meant that Jews were at a different level, they were subhuman. Cockroaches or beetles, perhaps, but not people. All of this happened before the ghetto and before the killings. We didn't understand it then, but in hindsight it was a prelude of things to come. If the Jews had suspected they were about to be put to death in their thousands, they might have tried to escape or hide. My father could have gotten us all out to the forest or perhaps hidden us with the help of some local Ukrainian farmers he knew – but he never did, because he never thought things would become so bad. Nobody did.

In October of 1941, several months after the Germans had invaded the area, they built the ghetto and imprisoned all the town's Jews. This was all a prelude to the mass killings. They took 3,500 Jews and crammed them into the space of several blocks. The Germans had it all planned out and were patiently waiting for the so-called extermination fruit to fully ripen. The idea was to be able to kill the Jews easily and face little to no resistance. This is why at first they implemented harsh decrees to wear them down. They then proceeded to imprison them, impose forced labor upon them, and in general terrorize and humiliate them. Finally, once they were frail and weak, they murdered them.

My parents were thirty-seven years old when they were murdered in the *Aktion* of July 25, 1942. My sister Buzha was only six years old. My paternal grandmother, Beila, was a strong woman who, it was thought, could only be killed by a cannon. Ultimately though, it was a German bullet that ended her life. She stayed with the family in the ghetto and was later murdered in the killing pits alongside my parents, my sister, and the rest of the family. My paternal grandfather Nusskin and my maternal grandmother Batya had both died prior to the war. My maternal grandfather, old man Fischman, traveled to Canada before the war and was thus saved from the atrocities. I never managed to locate him. My mother had very few relatives on her side of the family; not one of them made it out alive. I had five aunts and uncles on my father's side. Uncle Pesach survived the war after escaping a labor camp in Kostopil', but he was later killed by the Ukrainians. There were also Aunt Riva, Aunt Chaya, Aunt Miriam and Uncle Meir. Miriam and Meir were young and single, while the rest had children; they were all murdered in the pits. Try as I might, I no longer remember the names of all my cousins. I have a second cousin named Aryeh Koplik, who is also originally from Bereźne, and is the only other member of my family to survive the Holocaust. He came to Israel, worked as a cab driver, and built a family. His daughter Malka is named after his mother who perished in the Holocaust. Basically all of the Jews who survived, named their children after their murdered relatives. Aryeh fled the Kostopil' labor camp and hid in the forests like I did. His feet froze in the cold winters, and he had a limp to show for it his entire life. I remember he had a brother named Shmulik who didn't survive. We were the only two out of our entire family to make it out alive.

The Germans subjected the Jews in the ghetto to torture and forced labor. The Bereźne ghetto was not exclusive to locals; the Germans brought in Jews from the neighboring villages as well. This was their modus operandi wherever they went – gathering Jews from a large area into one centralized location, and keep them there in unbearably crowded conditions with scarce food, forced labor, and terror.

Most of the forced labor took place in Zirne, where there was a peat mine. The peat was used for energy and heat. Mining peat is incredibly hard work, and most of the Jews from the ghetto were sent there to work, my parents included. One day, my mother went to work and a German soldier tried to run her over with his motorcycle. It's entirely possible he was only trying to frighten her. They did that sort of thing a lot, the Germans – it was all fun and games to them. They enjoyed the intimidation and humiliation just as much as they enjoyed murdering. My mother had beautiful black hair, and I remember quite clearly that it was not too long after the Germans had arrived that it quickly turned gray.[1]

I was also frightened by a German soldier. I was climbing a pear tree to pick some fruit, and he pointed his pistol at me and said: "Jew boy, how dare you pick that pear?"

When the Germans came to town, they were drunk with victory after their triumphs against the Russians, and it showed in the way they treated the Jews. Shortly after their arrival they established the Ukrainian police, which was made up of nationalist individuals all too keen on collaborating with the Germans. Stepan Bandera was a prime example. He was one of the heads of the Ukrainian national movement, and was the chief leader and a hero to nationalist Ukrainians. The Germans promised them an independent Ukraine, liberated from the Russians whom they despised. This was the main reason for their collaboration with the Nazis; they also carried out many of the mass killings, as they also hated the Jews. Another example was

---

1. The phenomenon of relatively young people in the Holocaust whose hair quickly turned gray or white (sometimes even within hours) – due to the worry, the anxiety and the fear of death – is well documented.

a member of the Ukrainian police named Venke. After the war was over, I informed on him to the NKVD, the Russian secret police. He killed many Jews. Prior to the war he had been a coach driver for the registrar's office. When the Germans came, he enlisted along with many others in the Ukrainian police force. The Germans gave them uniforms and guns and they did the Germans' bidding. Those Ukrainians were the worst.

When the ghetto was established, you couldn't take any of your possessions with you, with the exception of what you were wearing at the time. So my mother dressed me in as many clothes as she could fit on me. I looked so fat because of all the clothes! She did the same to my only sister Batya. All the rest of our possessions remained in the house, and we were relocated to the ghetto. The ghetto itself was situated next to a stream, and we were placed in the building of a Torah school. They crammed the entire family into one room and gave us 200 grams of bread per day. My father would sneak into the Ukrainian villages and smuggle back some food from the farmers he used to trade with.

Eventually, for lack of food in the ghetto, my father placed me with a farmer named Soltus, who lived in Kurhany – about five or six miles from Bereźne. Thus there was one less mouth to feed in the ghetto and I had food and shelter. My father told him: "You keep my boy with you, feed him, and he will take your cows out to pasture. He's a clever boy." This is why I was saved – while the Jews were being slaughtered en masse, I was out in the fields with the cows. The farmer had a daughter named Lydia. She liked me and I liked her.

My sister stayed with my parents in the ghetto. I still wonder what might have been if my father had saved her too… I imagine how we might have escaped together if she had been with me in Kurhany. But she was still young, only about six or seven years old, and they didn't want to send her away. And so it was that she was murdered along with everyone else in the killing pits of Bereźne.

Before establishing the ghetto, some of the Germans still fraternized with the Jews. There were two beautiful young Jewish girls who caught the fancy of some of the German officers stationed in town. They slept with them and got them pregnant. When the officers found out they were pregnant, they took them to the graveyard and shot them. Why? Because they didn't want their superiors to find out what they had done, because mixing with inferior races was prohibited. I was taken along with several other children to cover their grave with earth. At the time it was a jolting experience for me, because this was before they had started murdering all the Jews. We had yellow badges, but there was no ghetto yet. When they built the ghetto they placed all the Jews in two or three blocks and the Ukrainians took their houses; the Germans had confiscated all their possessions, and whatever was left after taking what they wanted – they gave to the Ukrainians. The local gentiles were very antisemitic, but they never really hurt the Jews in the town, who were a large majority. The government also didn't condone it.

But the poor Ukrainian farmers were envious of the Jews' wealth. They suspected that the Jewish traders were cheating them, buying low and selling high, and it just didn't sit well with them. If we're being honest, it was actually true. The Jews ripped off the gentiles whenever they could. Ultimately the Ukrainians felt the Jews were exploiting them and they hated us for it.

As children we'd also play tricks on them. We'd put feces in a box and wrap it in foil to make the Ukrainians pick it up and open it. We liked to think we were getting back at them.

Ultimately, despite what may have been construed as several warning signs, we did not know that we would soon be led like lambs to the slaughter.

There had always been a foundation of antisemitism in Ukraine. There is no shortage of examples: as early as 1646, Ukrainian national hero Bohdan Khmelnytsky who led an uprising against the Poles, was a rabid antisemite. His men murdered many Jews during the battles with the Poles. In later years, during the Ukrainian uprisings against the Russians, there were multiple incidents of locals murdering Jews.

Ukraine is a very large country – 50 million residents who inhabit 250,000 square miles – but it has always been wedged between Russia and Poland. Indeed, at various times both the Russians and the Poles ruled the country. There was a famous Ukrainian poet named Taras Shevchenko who called for the establishment of an independent Ukrainian state, as early as the beginning of the 19th century. While this is of course a legitimate ambition, Ukrainian nationalist sentiment has always gone hand in hand with antisemitism and the murder of Jews. But nothing was ever as meticulous or calculated as the German killing machine. The German system was methodically led by government officials. Everything was mapped out and diligently calculated. They upgraded the murder of Jews from unorganized and sporadic to scientifically deliberate.

Each ghetto, city, and town – Berezne included – had a Jewish council called the "Judenrat". It was made up of individuals who cooperated with the Germans in false hope of preferential treatment. The Judenrat – particularly the Jewish Police, which was a department within it – was especially loathed by the ghetto's inhabitants. The head of the Jewish Police in Bereźne was a lawyer named Kremnitsky, and he was a bona-fide collaborator with the Germans. The Judenrat, much like the Capos in the concentration camps, were a tool the Germans used to control the Jews. The fact that they served the Germans' purpose didn't mean they were immune from their ultimate demise.

Our area was run by a German commander named Günther who lived in Kostopil', about 20 miles out of Bereźne. Whenever he came to town, there was a sense of fear. He was in charge of everything, including the murder of the Jews. There may have been no official document from Hitler ordering the extermination of all the Jews, but he spoke of it constantly. There's a famous speech of his from 1939, in which he said the Jews would pay the price if they caused a war to break out in Europe. Of course, later the Germans used the war as a pretext to kill all the Jews.

The Jews may not have suspected the Germans' intentions to eliminate them, but there was a sense of primal fear and apprehension. They knew things were bad, but deep down they didn't believe that the Germans were about to do what they ended up doing, because it had never happened this way before. There were always pogroms, but never mass murder. There were sporadic killings, but nothing systematic. And it didn't skip my family either: I had a cousin named Yonah Tabetchnik who was killed by the Ukrainians for courting one of their women. But it was another one of those incidents that was spontaneous rather than premeditated.

When the Germans came, they didn't start the killing straight away. The Jews took it a day at a time, and were hoping that the war would end soon. I remember traveling to the village with my father on business one day, and a farmer named Grubovych said to my father, "The Germans are on the march and Russia will fall." He was also an antisemite, even if he did trade with my father.

By sanctioning the killing of the Jews, Hitler rewarded the most primal instinct that exists within every man: the desire to kill. It has been around since Cain slew Abel. Human culture had put this desire under wraps, but now the Nazis had allowed the genie out of the bottle, so to speak, and murder in broad daylight was now basically approved by government. The Germans harnessed the antisemitic Ukrainians' hatred of the Jews and used it to help them do their bidding. Volyn Oblast had around 250,000 Jews before the war, and there were almost none left once the Germans were through. I, along with my fellow survivors who hid in the forests, managed to get out alive by chance. Even many of those who hid were later found and executed. The Ukrainians would either hand them over to the Germans or kill them directly.

During the time between the Germans' invasion in June 1941 and the murder of the Jews of Bereźne in 1942, we had heard rumors from Jewish refugees and even gentiles about the murder of Jews in Poland and the Soviet Union. We knew that Jews had been murdered throughout Volyn (in Rivne, for example) as early as the fall of 1941. The refugees told us of mass murders carried out by firing squad, of Jews being burned alive inside synagogues, and of gas chambers. And yet still, the Jews refused to believe that the Germans were capable of doing such things;

even if they were convinced of the atrocities that had befallen other Jews, they were in total denial about the possibility of the same happening to them. The Jewish mind is accustomed to thinking positive thoughts; it is inherently the mind of a good people – and it can't quite grasp the possibility of mass murder. The Jews always used to say, "We'll get through it, come what may." I'm convinced that if my father had believed that our entire family would be wiped out, he would have taken all of us into the forest, rather than sending me on my own to live with the farmer. He sent me there not so I would be saved from death, but so that there would be one less mouth to feed in the ghetto.[2]

In our town there was a poor Jew named Berl. I still remember his face; he had a long black beard. He lost his foot because of the cold, and he used to limp around on crutches with his legs wrapped in rags. He was an odd man, neglected and alone. He wasn't stupid, but he slurred his words and the townsfolk used to make fun of him. He would wander the streets day and night. I was told that he was killed one day by the Germans, even before the ghetto was built. He was walking the streets and most likely didn't acknowledge their call to halt. He was shot by "regular"

---

2. There were other reasons that Jews chose not to flee the ghetto, among them: the desire of a family to stay together – which greatly reduced the number of lone runaways; positive memories of the humane behavior of German soldiers in Poland during World War I; fear of the unknown associated with fleeing east; the sheer difficulty for the elderly and for children associated with undertaking such a quest; fear of treatment of refugees by the Russians; aerial attacks by the Luftwaffe on refugee convoys; and, of course, the inherent reluctance to leave one's home.

Wehrmacht, not SS. He was the first casualty of the German presence in Bereźne. It caused quite a shock. While the Jews knew that their lives were not held in the highest regard by the intruders, they never believed the mass killings were a possibility. After he was killed I remember being afraid and told my mother, "The Germans will kill us all." I was alert to the dangers, but my mother dismissed it, saying, "They only killed Berl because he was walking around at night. They won't kill everyone." She tried to allay my fears, but the incident left a mark on me. Thinking of my mother now brings great sorrow that she didn't get to see me grow up and accomplish things in life – build a family, write books… after all, all parents wish to see their children grow up and succeed. I like to think that perhaps my parents, in their dying moments, found solace in the fact that I had been saved from their own fate, and hoped that I would survive…

As I mentioned earlier, my father took me to a Ukrainian farmer named Soltus who lived in the village of Kurhany, near Bereźne. The main reason I was sent there was because of the severe lack of food in the ghetto, which was just as life-threatening as the Ukrainians or the Germans. My father knew Soltus well and he told him, "My boy will help you on the farm, and all you need to do is give him food and a place to sleep." Soltus agreed.

Deep down, I don't believe my parents ever believed the Germans would murder all the Jews, despite the terrible conditions and the dangers. They also probably thought I was safer in the village than in the ghetto, because there were no Germans on the farm. I wasn't happy about being sent there. I missed my family terribly, and one day I decided to go back to the

DR. SHAY EFRAT | 51

ghetto to see them. I brought a bag of peas back with me. The road from the village to the ghetto was not without its dangers, but I was a nimble young boy and more than capable of getting back on my own. I knew my way around. The distance from Kurhany to Bereźne was about 5 miles. I wore Ukrainian clothes, but I imagine anyone who saw me would know I wasn't Ukrainian. I remember how happy my sister Buzha was when she saw me. My father was out, and I asked my mother if I could stay with them in Bereźne. My mother started yelling at me to go back to Kurhany because they didn't have enough food, and I had enough food on the farm. I wanted so desperately to stay with them... I will never forget the smile on my sister's face when she saw me.

There was a barbed wire fence around the ghetto, patrolled by the Jewish Police. They wore armbands with a Star of David and always tried to curry favor with the Germans. After staying briefly with my mother and sister, I snuck back out through a small opening in the fence and escaped back to Kurhany, and luckily I wasn't caught. I assume they wouldn't have killed me on the spot if they'd caught me, but I would surely have been beaten. They hadn't started killing us yet at the time. A local once killed a Jew and the Germans reprimanded him, saying "only we kill the Jews". They were well organized, the Germans. First they starved us of food, imposed forced labor on us, and then tortured us. Only once we were weak and famished would they begin the killing. But once the murders started, any Ukrainian could murder a Jew at any moment with impunity. A Jewish life was worth less than that of a dog. Dogs weren't being killed for no reason, but Jews were. Death was lurking at every turn.

# CHAPTER 3:
# SURVIVAL OF THE HUNTED

The Germans' method for murdering the Jews was simple: they would gather everyone from the ghetto, assemble them at a convenient location such as the town square or a large building, and then march them to the killing area and murder them by shooting them in large pre-dug pits. They were usually shot naked, meaning they were first forced to strip, and the Germans or their Ukrainian henchmen would take the clothes. The Bereźne killings began on August 25, 1942, and lasted two days. The pits were dug near the graveyard by the Ukrainians the night before, at the behest of the Germans. They dug three large pits, and in the morning the Jews were rounded up, marched to the pits, and told to strip as one final humiliation. They were then forced to lie down in the pits, where they were shot from above. The operation was overseen by the SS. The people who did the actual killing were German policemen and SS soldiers along with Ukrainian militia members. The babies and small children were generally tossed into the pits and weren't even shot; they died from suffocation. That was another thing the Germans tended to do, they found it a waste of bullets to shoot a baby who would die anyway. Many people were shot but did not die straight away, and lay dying a horrible death for hours or even days in the pits.

In two days the Germans killed 3,680 Jews, while I was out in the fields with the cows – the reason I was saved. I often think about my sister. I wonder who was shot first, her or my mother. If I had been in the town that day, I would not have made it out alive.

A few years ago, I traveled to Bereźne with my wife Bracha, and my sons Natan and Yotam. We visited Soltus's house, the farmer, my Ukrainian host in Kurhany where I stayed at while the killings were going on, and we actually saw his daughter Lydia – she is already very old. She recognized me and said, "That's Sucha – the boy who tended to our cows." I was so moved! I had loved her as a boy, she was a beautiful young Ukrainian woman.

Modern-day Bereźne is very pretty. We visited the memorial next to the site of the mass grave where all those Jews met their demise. I gave a little speech. There are two tombstones by the site of the three pits. One of them was placed there by the Russian government and reads "At this site 3,680 citizens of the Soviet Union were murdered by the Fascist Nazis." The other was erected by the Bereźne survivors, and includes the Hebrew words from a poem by Alterman: "And our blood in small vases you collected because no one else would, only you alone." My entire family is in those pits!

As far as I know, there were no survivors from the shootings. The details we know of from those two days, we heard from Ukrainian eyewitnesses who, once the war was over, told the Jews what had happened. They said that one man cried out, "Run for your lives!" and was immediately gunned down, and thereafter no one else dared speak up or try to flee… I often think of my father, who was only thirty-seven years old, and a strapping, strong man he was! He had served in the Polish army and had many contacts among the local gentiles. He could have found a way to escape with the family or to resist… I find it hard to accept that they died without a fight. I understand it logically, but emotionally it is a bitter pill to swallow. When I found out about the killings, I was in the house of the farmer who took me in. I was sad, but I was just a young boy. I wasn't fully aware of the situation, and I was too preoccupied with my own day-to-day survival. Years later, once I grew older and processed the profound loss, I truly felt the sadness and grief. It is a feeling that only intensifies with time – when you're a young man, you act like one – always busy and responsive to whatever life throws at you. The older you get, the more time you have to think – and to remember…

On the day the Jews were murdered at Bereźne, I was out in the fields with the cows. I was singing and hopping around like a little Ukrainian. In the evening, when I got back to the farmer's house, I noticed several farmers whispering amongst themselves, taking care not to let me overhear them. They sat at the front of the house on little benches, as they did every evening, but this time when they saw me they lowered their voices. Obviously they were whispering about the killings, but I heard them. Later, after the war was over, one of the farmers told me that when my mother and sister were walking toward the killing pits, my sister was thirsty and the Ukrainian guards would not let her or any of the other Jews have water. He told me that my mother took off her ring and gave it to them so that they might let them have some water. I don't know whether the story is true, but that's what he told me. At the farmer's house, I always slept next to the farmer's son, whose name was Nikola. We used to sleep on bales of hay. Nikola was a delicate young boy, and that night he wept because of all the Jews that had been killed.

Several days later, the Germans issued a *Meldung* (announcement) and posted it at the village offices: "Any Jew who is found by local citizens must be turned over to the authorities. Anyone caught hiding Jews is liable to be executed, and his house will be demolished..." Soltus the farmer, my Ukrainian host was alarmed by the edict and came to me one morning, saying, "I am afraid of the Germans and you must leave." He gave me some bread and sent me into the forest. He directed me to hide out there and told me that he would come in the night and bring me food, which he never did.

Soltus's house was situated at the edge of the village, and near his house was a relatively small birch tree forest. I remember how terrified I was walking in there for the first time. I scurried about like a frightened rabbit, crying and yelling... finally, I instinctively fell silent so I would not be heard. At that moment I thought I was the last Jewish boy remaining in the world. I stayed in the forest for quite a few days and nights. The forest was small and dense, and at first I couldn't find anything to eat. To find food, I would leave the forest and go knocking on the doors of farmers I knew (and even some I didn't know), begging, "Please, good people. Could you spare some food for a young orphan?" Some of them gave me food. Others sent me away, often cursing at me, "Dirty Jew, get out of here!" Sometimes they would threaten to turn me over to the Germans. On one of those first few days in the forest I had a very close call. I didn't know any better and went looking for food in broad daylight. A farmer who was chopping wood saw me and started chasing me with his axe. When he caught me I soiled my pants in fright! He grabbed me with one hand, brandished the axe with the other and said: "You miserable Jew, go away and don't come back!" I assume he just wanted to scare me, because he could easily have killed me right then and there. Maybe he felt sorry for me, I couldn't say for sure. What I do know is that there were multiple incidents of farmers killing Jews who were hiding or looking for food. They would use an axe or a pitchfork or a sickle or a scythe. Sometimes they would shoot them. There was the occasional good-hearted farmer who would give me a piece of bread or a potato, and I would scurry off like an animal. Sometimes I would steal the food they brought with them when they were out harvesting crops. They would bring a basket with food, and while they were working I would sneak up, grab what I could and run off.

I once met a Ukrainian woman in a field at the edge of the forest. I asked her for food but she looked at me and said, "Come to my house and I'll feed you." I was famished, and wanted nothing more than to eat, but I was uncertain whether I should go with her – I was afraid she might turn me over to the Germans or kill me. I saw a bird standing on the branch of a tree nearby. I decided that if the bird stayed on the branch I would go with her, and if it flew away I would not. I waited for a bit, and suddenly the bird took off in flight… I turned around and went back into the forest.

After a while I learned that I could find food in the forest as well. There were all sorts of seeds, berries, and mushrooms. Occasionally I would find little sparrow eggs, or larger crow eggs which I would steal from their nests. Most people, especially these days, find this reality hard to grasp – but those are the things I had to do in order to survive.

After Soltus sent me away, I never dared go back to his house. I never met a single Jew in that forest, and I was all alone. At night I slept on the forest floor and used to imagine all sorts of things. As a young boy, the trees looked like people to me – bigger trees were men, smaller trees were women, and the smallest trees and bushes were children. After several days or weeks – I'm not so sure of the timeline anymore – I summoned up some courage and went to a farmer from Kurhany whom I knew quite well from the days he used to trade with my father. I had even been at his house several times before the Holocaust. He was a tall Pole named Henrik, and he agreed to give me some food and let me sleep on a bale of hay in the barn. Almost every house in the village had a barn, and the barn always had bales of hay. Henrik was a good man. His wife was Ukrainian and I remember he had a chronic cough. He grew tobacco next to the barn and he used to smoke cigarettes constantly. When I got there I found out there was a Jewish woman already there in hiding. Her name was Tony and she was staying there with her little boy, Hershele. While we stayed there, if we had to go to the toilet we would do it in the corner, wipe ourselves with hay and discard the waste outdoors… we could not leave the barn for fear of being seen. Tony also survived the Holocaust, and eventually immigrated to Israel. Years later my wife Bracha and I visited her at her home in Kiryat Haim near Haifa. Before the Holocaust she had had five children, but when I met her at Henrik's barn all she had left was little Hershele. The Germans and Ukrainians had killed everyone else. She told me, "If it weren't for Hershele, I would have already been dead... I only stayed alive for the boy." A while later Hershele died in the forest, and she struggled for survival and ultimately stayed alive. I remember once while we were in the barn, I laughed about something – just an innocent boy's laugh. She reacted so fiercely she scratched my face until it bled, exclaiming, "All those Jews have been killed and you're laughing?!" We stayed there for a few days until Henrik came and told us that the Germans had threatened to execute anyone caught hiding a Jew. "You must leave," he told us, and so we left...

After leaving Henrik's farm, I split up with Tony and Hershele and decided to continue on my own. For reasons which are still unclear to me, I chose to leave the Kurhany area and trekked north towards the villages of Polyany and Bronne. I dared not return to Bereźne, assuming that in such a large place there were sure to be many Germans – and, after all, that was where all the Jews were murdered. I spent most of my time hiding in the forests, because venturing out in broad daylight was extremely dangerous. However, I still had trouble finding food, and I still had to go searching for food in the villages. I encountered the same responses there as well – some would give me some bread or potatoes, most of the others would turn me away. The worst ones would say, "Damn Jew, get away before I kill you or hand you over to the Germans." Most Ukrainians – and many Poles as well – were very antisemitic even before the war. They always envied the Jews, saying things like "Look at them in their fancy suits eating rich, white bread while we eat brown bread and dress in rags." They would constantly complain about the "blood-sucking Jews". I remember a young Polish boy telling me to "go to Palestine". The environment was very antisemitic. So when I was hiding out in the forests, I felt like I was a two-legged animal being hunted. There were many times where I was close to giving up, especially during the lonely, dark nights. I had no one to talk to, and to avoid going insane I would talk to trees and bushes and rocks and animals. Again, I thought I must be the last Jewish boy alive in the world. I prayed to God, but of course he didn't answer. I finally decided to help myself and go searching for other Jews.

I'm not sure how long I remained in hiding by myself. It might have been a few weeks, it might have been less. I was now actively searching for Jews, because I had heard that there were some who had managed to escape and were hiding out in the forests or the villages. Gradually they began to form groups. One day a kind-hearted farmer told me about a group of Jews hiding out nearby. After much searching I managed to locate the group hiding in the Bronne forest, about ten miles north of Bereźne. When I visited Bereźne with my wife, children, and grandchildren, I showed them the location of the forest – but we didn't go inside. There were maybe 40 or 50 Jews who had escaped and were hiding out in Bronne forest. They welcomed me and I joined them, staying with them for several months.

In order to survive, we would do things which would be hard to grasp nowadays. We used to take clothes hanging from clotheslines, steal chickens from the farmyards, or steal the food the farmers would bring with them for lunch in the fields. One

ingredient which was in very short supply was salt. One day I
went looking for food in the fields. I saw a Polish farmer's house,
and next to it was what appeared to be a bag of salt. I licked it to
be sure, and while it was salty – it was decidedly *not* salt. It was
in fact a sort of chemical fertilizer. I stole the bag and we used
that to cook potatoes with, and even though it was chemical
fertilizer, nothing happened to us...I remember it well – this
Polish farmer was ahead of his time. He used chemical fertilizer
rather than organic manure. Incidentally, salt was in short supply
not only amongst the Jews hiding in the forest, but amongst the
farmers as well. The Germans would use this as incentive – they
made it known that any local gentile who handed over a Jew
to the authorities would be given three kilograms of salt as a
reward. It became common for a Ukrainian farmer's wife to tell
her husband, "We're short of salt, go catch a Jew and get us some
salt from the Germans."

Those days I was still relatively inexperienced, and one
evening I committed a grave error which very nearly resulted
in my demise. It was much safer to be out in the dark, so I
knocked on the door of a farmer's house and asked for food.
The farmer and his wife were kind to me, especially the wife
who was breastfeeding a baby while half naked. When I went
in the farmer was eating, and being famished as I was, I started
watering at the mouth. They gave me some food and said, "You
can sleep on our pantry floor tonight. In the morning you can
eat breakfast with us and then you'll leave." I was extremely tired
and finally well fed, was not aware of the danger. I fell asleep
quickly, awoke the next morning, and sat down for breakfast.
As I was eating, the farmer suddenly grabbed me, tied my hands

with a rope and put me in his cart. He was taking me to Bereźne to hand me over to the Germans and collect his reward… about halfway there I began to cry. I knew the road well, and I realized that as we drew nearer to the town, I was getting closer and closer to death. I wailed and cried until he said, "Why are you crying?" I told him I had to pee, I was about to wet my pants and it hurt to hold it in. I swore to him that's all I needed to do. I kept begging him and he did not know what to do, until finally he gave in and told me to go under a tree. He untied me and I seized the opportunity and escaped. He tried to catch me at first, but I was much quicker and managed to get away. After the war I contacted the NKVD, the Russian secret police, and turned him over. I told them, "This man killed Jews and he almost killed me." I narrowly escaped death several times, and I started to think that perhaps I was immortal…

The Ukrainian farmers collaborated with the Germans for multiple reasons: firstly, we'd steal food and other items necessary for our survival, such as clothes. Secondly, the vast majority of Ukrainians were inherently antisemitic to begin with, and were happy to get rid of the Jews. Thirdly, the Germans rewarded them for every Jew they killed or turned in, with money or food – especially salt which was notoriously hard to acquire. Fourthly, anyone who helped the Jews was in fact endangering his own and his family's life. All of these reasons served as motivation for the Ukrainians to get rid of us.

Our group in the forest included ten armed Jews who would rob the Ukrainians of their cows and sheep at gunpoint. They were nicknamed "The Ten". The Ukrainians decided to take revenge and divulged our hiding place to the Germans.

In the cold, snowy winter of 1942-1943, the Germans enlisted the Ukrainians' help and ambushed us. The Ukrainians were the most dangerous because they knew the forests and weren't afraid to go inside them, unlike the Germans who most certainly were. Those Germans weren't the bravest men… occasionally they would assemble their forces and would venture into the forests with their Ukrainian guides to hunt Jews. They called it "Oblava" - which is Russian for "raid".

One day, the Germans showed up with Ukrainian militiamen and Hungarian soldiers (another of the Germans' allies), surrounded the forest and conducted a raid. They took us by surprise, shooting from all directions. We scattered and ran, but we were surrounded. To this day I'm not sure how I survived. The forest was divided into areas called "quartels" which had pathways between them in order to facilitate hunting or lumberjacking. The Germans and Hungarians came from the pathways, shot at us from all sides and killed many of us. I understood that if I kept running, I would be killed, and so I fell into the snow and played dead. The Germans had big dogs in order to sniff us out. One of the dogs grabbed me from behind and began to drag me by the seat of my pants. The dog and the German soldier could tell I was alive… but for some reason – perhaps he was queasy at the sight of blood – he did not kill me. He took his dog and left, and I survived. After the ambush, the survivors in our group split up. Some went northwest to the forest of Karachun, about 17 miles northwest of Bereźne. The forest was named after the adjacent Polish village. The nationalist Ukrainian partisans expelled or killed the local Poles. They hated the Poles for the same reason they hated the

Russians: they viewed them as a despised foreign ruler. I went to Karachun, along with several of the survivors of the ambush.

At the edge of Karachun was the house of a farmer – I don't remember his name – who took us in and gave us shelter until the next morning. I remember I was completely frozen from all the snow and he placed me on a big baking oven he had in his home, and I sat there until I thawed through and dried off. When we left the farmer's house the next morning on our way to the forest, we encountered serious trouble.

Next to the village we ran into a group of Ukrainian partisans nicknamed "The Banderas" because they were loyal to Stepan Bandera, the Ukrainian nationalist leader. They dreamed of an independent Ukraine and fought alongside the Germans against the Russians, and were happy to participate in the murder of the Jews. They yelled at us, "Stoy!" (Stop) and started shooting. Bullets were whistling through the air all around us. Chaim, a young man who was standing right next to me, was hit. He cried out "Mama!" and fell to the ground, dead. I still remember his face. We leaped for cover and lay in the bushes. We could hear the German trains not far from there. We lay low until dusk and then entered the Karachun forest under cover of darkness. We managed to get away and finally we found another group of Jews in hiding and joined up with them.

Most of my time between the murder of the Jews in Bereźne and the liberation of the area by the Russian army was spent in the Karachun forest. It was a big, deep forest and we felt relatively safe in it. In fact, all the forests I stayed in weren't far away from Bereźne. At first I stayed in the forest near the farmer's house in Kurhany, about 6 miles west of Bereźne. I then moved to the Bronne forest about 10 miles northwest of Bereźne, and finally to Karachun forest, about 20 miles northwest of Bereźne. There were all sorts of Jews hiding in Karachun forest. Among them were the Brayer family, with whom I was very close until liberation. The family now lives in Israel. They hid with me in the forests, and we left the forests together once the area had been liberated. Most of the family survived. Years later my wife Bracha and I visited them at their home in Bat Yam. There were the brothers Shalom and Yosele Brayer, their sister Henya Brayer, and their father Avraham Brayer – who was later murdered when he went looking for food. Many Jews were murdered when they were out looking for food, but I survived. At the time I believed that I was chosen by God to live and tell the tale. I thought I was immortal; as if I were destined to live. There were many dangers, many killings – and I always managed to escape. Evading the Germans and the Ukrainians as a Jew was no mean feat. One had to survive, while being constantly hunted, for almost eighteen months in the forests – from August 1942 until January 1944, when the Russian 13th Army finally liberated the area. From about January 1943 to January 1944, which accounted for the majority of my stay in Karachun forest, I was with a close friend of mine. His name was Baruch Kopyt. He was about my age, and was originally from the village of Zdolbuniv near Rivne. He also survived the war and immigrated to Israel. Despite trying for many years, I never managed to locate him. I only have one picture of him, riding a bike with Yosele Brayer at the Föhrenwald displaced persons camp in Germany after the war. When the Russian army liberated the area in early 1944, we left the forest and he said, "I'm going back to Zdolbuniv to see if there's anyone left of my family." I returned to Bereźne and then went to the military boarding school in Kursk. Later someone told me that he had joined the Hashomer Hatzair youth movement and came to Israel, but still I could never track him down. Baruch and I were quite the pair! We would steal food from the farmers together... Shalom Brayer wrote a book of memoirs titled "The Kostopil' Uprising", where he mentioned us both as "Shmuel and Baruch Kopyt, the adopted sons of Gedalya Erlich". Gedalya was a sort of surrogate father for us in the forest. He was an older Jew with no family who cared for us and took us under his wing. Kostopil' is a town around 20 miles southwest of Bereźne. Approximately 400 Jews were kept there and forced to work in the peat mines for the Germans. On the day of the Bereźne massacre, they were about to be killed as well when they led an uprising and fled. Some of them managed to make it into the forests and lived. Among them was my uncle Pesach, who was later murdered by the Ukrainians after liberation.

The Ukrainian and Polish farmers were mostly antisemitic. They would blame the Jews for killing Jesus, and urge them to "go to Palestine", telling them that "this is not your country". The Germans always made use of local collaborators wherever they went. They fueled the fires of antisemitism, resentment, and envy of the gentiles, and also provided financial incentives for the locals to be rid of the Jews by offering their possessions and their jobs. This caused many Jews to be murdered by the local gentiles, whether in an organized or unorganized fashion. Jewish lives were worth less than a dog's life during those times. That's why I was always jealous of dogs. They may have been tied up, but they had food, a home, and security. I had none of those and could be killed at any moment.

The Jews in the forest lived in a sort of improvised "family campsite". Most of the people there – such as the Kessler family, the Brayer family and Gedalya Erlich (my adopted father) – were from Bereźne. Some of them I knew from before the war. There were also several Jews from villages near Bereźne, and a few from places further away. My good friend Baruch Kopyt and I lived together with Gedalya in the same "burrow" and were extremely close to him. I remember that he, like others in the group, carried a Russian rifle, but he wasn't part of the partisans. He was originally from the Carpathian mountainous area in southern Ukraine, bordering Romania. Quite a few Jews came from there during the population transfer[3] conducted by the Russians after they captured the area from the Romanians in 1940. They sent the local Germans back to Germany and brought in Poles and Ukrainians to take their place; however, there were also several Jews who were transferred and moved to our area, and that was how Gedalya arrived in Bereźne.

We weren't Partisans, and in our group there was no one who had actually fought the Germans. Consequently, our group was not a group of partisan fighters, but rather a group of escapees – some of whom were armed for self-defense against the Germans

---

3. During and after World War II, the Soviet Union used to alter the borders between countries it had conquered in order to expand the territory of the USSR. Subsequently, it also engaged in the transfer of millions of people from place to place in order to adjust the population in accordance with the new borders.

and the hostile Ukrainians. Several people managed to secure weapons – mostly semi-automatic rifles, which allowed for a certain sense of security. When the Russian army retreated in July 1941, they left many weapons in the area. The farmers collected some of them and the Jews then either bought or traded for most of their weapons. When we left the forest after the Russians had liberated the area, they hid the firearms under the bushes in the snow and left them there. They didn't want the Russians to see Jews with rifles and mistake us for nationalist partisans loyal to the Germans. I remember as a young boy I had an old broken rifle. I would proudly wear it on my shoulder and march through the camp. Of course it was only a toy, it didn't really work. I don't really remember ever meeting any Partisans, though I had heard quite a lot about them. Colonel Medvedev's partisan battalion – which had a few Jews – was situated near Rivne. There were several other partisan brigades and battalions scattered throughout the occupied areas of the Soviet Union. The most famous partisan commander was Sydir Kovpak. His brigade also had a Jewish platoon. His brigade fought the Germans mainly in the mountainous region of Carpatoros, far away from the areas I hid in. The partisans were closely linked with the Russian Red Army and were de facto a part of it. They received weapons and guidance and were organized just like an army. However, rather than fight on the front lines, they fought the Germans behind enemy lines and caused a lot of damage. Several German generals said that the partisans were one of the main reasons they lost the war in eastern Europe. They were a thorn in the Germans' side – sabotaging railway lines, ambushing German units, liberating prisoner camps and more… they killed many, many German soldiers and severely damaged their morale. No matter how hard they tried, the Germans could not find a way to outfox the partisans from a military standpoint.

Looking back, it's hard to say there was anything I liked about the forest as a boy. Life was extremely difficult and dangerous, even though I did feel a certain element of safety and had a little bit of food. Ultimately though, I still have a love of nature and the forest. It was what sheltered us from the Germans as they almost never ventured inside, with the exception of the occasional raid. The Ukrainians weren't as afraid and we had to be more careful of them.

Our camp didn't have any leadership per se. The older men gave guidance but there was not organized leadership. People organized by family or other groupings, and each group had their own "burrow" – Ziblanka" in Russian. We were like a pack of wolves living together. Each man for himself, but as a group. It was a group of families who joined with lone individuals gathered from all sorts of places, like myself. There was no particular schedule we kept, no specific time to get up. We woke up in the morning and went searching for food – whether in the forest, or begging and stealing from the local farmers. We would move alone or in small groups. Upon reflection, our daily lives weren't too different from that of an animal: get up, go out and look for food. Survive. We never really had enough to eat. Even if you had a tiny bit of food, you had to save some for later.

I don't remember exactly how many children there were in our group, but there couldn't have been many more than ten. There were the Brayers, the Kesslers, Baruch Kopyt, myself, and a few others. Our camp didn't have any old people or infants. They had such slim chances of surviving in the forest. The oldest people in our group were about thirty years old; the youngest were about ten or twelve. There were about 35 or 40 people in the group.

There wasn't much of an effort to educate the children or to have studies, because the children were an integral part of the food search and survival effort. On summer nights when we used to sit together, some of the older men told some stories, but that was it. We'd sit around the fire together, talking, singing, and roasting potatoes. People would tell jokes and stories of their adventures evading danger and acquiring food. We just lived what lives we had. We couldn't just be sad and cry. Each day we would gather mushrooms in the forest and various items from the farmers' fields, but it was never enough. We always had to go looking for food inside the villages and come in direct contact with the locals, who more often than not were hostile. The farmers in the Polish villages usually gave us food, mostly pieces of bread or some potatoes. Those Ukrainians who gave us food weren't as generous as the Poles, and of course there were always those (mostly Ukrainians but Poles too) who tried to capture Jews to turn them over to the Germans – or kill them directly. Some of our people were murdered when they were out looking for food. The risk of death was ever present, and we were all preoccupied first and foremost with survival. Thus there was no time or real desire for things like studies. But people did need company, culture, and laughter. We were a small community of sorts, living together and – beyond the most pressing need for survival – trying to create some kind of culture. Sometimes people would pray together on the holidays and I remember some people fasted on Yom Kippur, but that was all.

Other than evading the hostile locals and the Germans, our main challenges in the forest were hunger, cold and lice. I remember wearing clothes made of thin flannel called "Leibel" that my mother had given me when I went to live with the farmer in Kurhany. I wore them for two years until we left the forest, and they were always full of lice. It was impossible to get rid of them, and I had the most horrible itch! They laid their eggs in the folds on the stitches and multiplied constantly. They were little yellow creatures with tiny legs, and we would crush them with our fingernails. Even washing the clothes in the summer when it was warm didn't really help. Avraham Brayer told us that when he served in the Austrian army, they would place their clothes by the fire and the lice would fall off. We did that and it helped to an extent, but the lice always came back. It was a never ending war, and due to lacking the most basic elements of rudimentary hygiene, the lice always won.

I remember I had shoes that I had brought with me from home, but after a while they were ripped and too small for my feet because I was a growing young boy. In the forest we wrapped our feet in rags, and we'd weave makeshift shoes called "Postals" from the birch tree bark. The Ukrainian villagers used to do the same and wrap them in wool, but we of course had to do without the wool. We used rags so our feet wouldn't freeze in the snow...

Drinking water was never a problem, as there is abundant water in Ukraine. It rains all the time, even in the summer, and the ground is saturated with water. Unlike in Israel, fields are watered using only rainwater. No matter where you are, if you dig a hole two feet deep, you'll find water. At first it's muddy, but soon enough you'll get cool, clear drinking water. Moreover, in the forest there are many streams and brooks with clear running water, so being thirsty was never an issue. We'd also cut a notch in the birch tree bark and extract the sweet nectar. We'd collect wild berries and button mushrooms from the forests, peas and potatoes from the farmers' fields. I remember our camp had a big pot which we used to cook potatoes and whatever else we could find. We lit the fire with matches we got from the farmers. We didn't have many matches, so we used to cut them in half and always kept the fire burning. Deep in the woods we felt more or less safe, so we weren't afraid to light a fire, despite the smoke in the day and the light at night. We didn't have people guarding the camp round the clock. I assume it was because they thought the Germans wouldn't reach us so deep in the forest, but I was only a boy and I can't be sure that is the reason.

We weren't afraid of animals in the forest. I know there were bears and wolves, but I don't recall ever running into them. We'd hear the wolves howling at night. They may have been dangerous, but I don't remember ever hearing of a Jew being devoured by a wolf. The real danger was the humans – especially when we ventured out to look for food. We usually went in groups of two or three. There was no organized structure or schedule, people just organized on their own and went to look for food. They usually went out during the night, because hanging around the villages in broad daylight was extremely dangerous. Many Jews were caught and killed because they went out looking for food during the day. At first we didn't know any better, but after gaining some experience, we learned that it was only reasonable to venture out at night.

This was our life – the farthest thing from normal you could imagine. It's hard to grasp, I am fully aware. People listening to these stories today would have a hard time comprehending them. But such was life for us – a Jew's life was worthless. Our entire existence in the forests was survival of the hunted. And despite not having any central organizational structure, ours was a cohesive group and conducted itself based on certain moral codes. For example, I can't remember any incidents of people stealing food from each other.

One of the more challenging issues we had was that of hygiene. Of course we had no showers, and we didn't dare go bathe in the river – it was just too risky. In fact, I didn't shower for eighteen months. In the summer you could rinse yourself off in the rain or in the streams. When it got hot, we used to use the ash from the birch trees and would rub it with some water on our bodies. The ash has a form of caustic soda in it, and mixing it with water creates a sort of natural soap. But most of the time we were covered in a permanent layer of grime, which at least protected us somewhat from the cold in the winter. We relieved ourselves in nature – each person found their own spot, there were obviously no toilets. We couldn't wash our hands after, either, because there wasn't anything to do it with. We used leaves to wipe ourselves. The girls would go farther away than the boys, and sometimes we'd sneak a peek from afar. We had no medicine at all. We had some "natural cures" we used in lieu of medication, but in general if you got sick, you just had to find a way to get better. We had one doctor in our group who went by the name of Bornstein, but he had no medicine or any other means of medical treatment. The best we could do was consult with him as to what we could do with the limited means we had. But despite these shortages, our group was made up of strong people – not one person died due to disease. I remember once during Yom Kippur Eve prayers in the forest, one young man just collapsed and died, most likely of a heart attack.

The dirt and lack of hygiene caused some bad cases of scabies. It brings about a terrible uncontrollable itch which results in pus-filled pimples. I remember Yosele Brayer suffered terribly from it, and his father Avraham managed to get him some ointment from one of the farmers. I was lucky enough not to catch it. I was actually not sick at all during my time in the forest.

No one changed clothes because there was no change of clothes. The men didn't shave and the women didn't apply makeup or color their hair. There was only survival.

One of the worst things was of course the cold winter. Temperatures in the Ukrainian winter can reach as low as -13 °F, and I had to endure two such winters between 1942 and 1944. At those temperatures, your spit freezes before it reaches the ground, and when you urinate it freezes upon contact with the earth. We built what we called "burrows". It wasn't an underground burrow, but a small, short structure where you could only stand in the middle but had to bend down at the sides. We built them with tree branches partially dug into the ground. We'd cover the branches with dirt and moss and would leave one side open as the entrance. We'd light a fire inside to keep warm, and the embers always burned. There was a lot of smoke but it's how we kept warm; without a fire, we would never have survived. We slept inside on piles of straw or old burlap sacks we found. We covered ourselves in the same sacks in lieu of blankets. I didn't even have a coat throughout my time in the forest! I managed to steal some clothes from the clotheslines in the Ukrainian villages, but I never found a proper coat. Nevertheless, I managed to survive two bitterly cold winters!

I remember at our camp at Karachun, there were several single young men and several pretty young women, but I don't know if anything ever happened, romantically speaking. As a boy, I tended not to notice those things. I remember there were some young men who courted the women, who usually weren't too keen to oblige. There were rumors of boys in the group who had relationships with some of the Ukrainian women in the surrounding villages whose husbands had been killed or enlisted, although I can't be sure those rumors are true. There may have been someone in our group who later married a Ukrainian woman. In any event, there were no babies born in our group during our time there. Sexuality did exist, I'm sure, but I didn't notice it as much. When a man is under constant threat of death, he doesn't have much time for those things. First he must survive, and then he must secure food. Only if he feels safe and satisfied, can he think of women sexually.

During our time in the forest, we were apprised by the farmers of the situation on the frontlines, which helped us maintain some form of optimism. We always had hope, because without hope there is no life. When the Germans began to withdraw, we cheered up and reminded ourselves why it was worth making the effort to survive. And so we did, even if despair crept in on occasion. The intense desire to live keeps a man alive. It is a sort of compass that directs one to strive for life. In our group, not one person committed suicide – despite the immense pain and despair. We kept busy trying to survive. There were stories of suicides that happened after the war was over. There were two main things that kept me hopeful: one was that the Russians would prevail and we would be saved; the other was that I might find someone from my family who had survived. This was always my hope; it was my fellow Jews' hope as well. The desire to tell my story and the need for revenge also crossed my mind, but not as much during my time in the forest. Those came after we were liberated. But the thing that helped me survive more than anything else was the basic human instinct to exist. It is that instinct that pushes one to make a superhuman effort to survive. The body yearns to keep living, as does the soul; both of these make up the whole that is a human. And a human as such wishes dearly to continue existing, even in the face of incomprehensible hardship and continuous suffering such as we experienced in the Holocaust every single day.

# CHAPTER 4:
# LIBERATION AND VENGEANCE


Most of the Jews who survived in eastern Poland and Ukraine did so by means of hiding in the forest. We were lucky that Ukraine has so many forests! There were precious few that were saved thanks to kind-hearted locals who hid them in their homes. There were also those who joined the Soviet partisans and were saved if they were not killed in battle. Those few who had the foresight to escape when the German invasion began were also saved, for the most part.

Our area was liberated by the great 13th Army of the Soviet Red Army, commanded by General Nikolai Pukhov. I researched this in great detail. When I traveled to Bereźne several years ago I also went to Rivne, a large city about 37 miles southwest of Bereźne. There's a Red Army Museum there, and I saw quite a few photos and documents about the 13th Army and its commander General Pukhov.

An Army is a military formation which includes ten or twelve divisions and numbers around 150,000 soldiers. The 13th Army was part of the Soviet forces which fought the Germans at the "First Ukrainian Front" – the northwest of Ukraine, which includes Volyn Oblast and my hometown of Bereźne. The liberation of our group in the forest took place on or around January 10, 1944. Cutting through the Karachun forest in which we were holed up was a railroad crossing east to west from Russia. The Germans had been using it to transport military supplies and troops. On that day in January, we suddenly heard loud cannon fire. We were wondering what was happening when the trains stopped abruptly and we saw Red Army reconnaissance troops, followed closely by infantry troops. They marched on the railroad like black ants, masses of troops as far as the eye could see... they were everywhere! I remember Shalom Brayer telling me to kiss and hug the first Russian I saw. He did the same, and the bewildered Russian soldier yelled, "What are you doing?!" I also remember an "older" Russian soldier – he must have been about forty or fifty – who smugly asked me as I walked out of the forest, "How far to Berlin?" He strutted about like a peacock with his rifle slung over his shoulder.

Among the Russian soldiers, there were also young boys and older men, at least forty years old; the Russians drafted anyone who could fight. The soldiers were armed with rifles held by ropes in lieu of straps, wearing faded, ripped, and frayed uniforms, and carrying small backpacks. In those backpacks there was some food – mostly canned goods and crackers that the Russians had received from the Americans.[4] They saw we were hungry and gave us some food. I mainly remember the canned pork that they gave us.

---

4. As part of the "Lend-Lease" Act, during the war the United States supplied the Soviets with vast amounts of equipment – including arms, food, medicine, clothes, and more. This equipment was sent in large shipments and was instrumental in the successful effort by the Russians to stall the Germans, and indeed to the Soviet victory at large. This equipment was in fact a gift, as the Soviets never repaid the Americans.

Upon seeing the Russians, I truly felt like I had crossed from darkness into light! Hiding out in the woods is akin to darkness, as you are in permanent concealment. Leaving the forest was akin to being bathed in light. It is nearly impossible to describe the intense feeling of relief and liberation, and the realization that you no longer need to cower like a frightened animal. This is why I so fondly remember who it was that liberated us – the great 13th Army.

When we walked out of the forest I began to cry. A Russian officer – who also happened to be Jewish – asked me, "We just liberated the area. What are you crying for?!" I told him I want to go and serve in the army to fight the Germans and avenge my family. The officer said, "But you're only a boy – you can't join the military!"

Once we were liberated, those in our group who were from Bereźne wanted to go back home. The others wanted to go back to their own villages and towns. We all wanted to find out if there was anyone in our families who had survived. We walked toward Bereźne, stopping on the way in various abandoned villages to look for food and other items. Eventually we arrived in Bereźne, and each of us went to his former home to see if anybody had come back, and what had become of the house. In most cases, the houses were now occupied by Ukrainians, and nobody had come back. When I got to our house, I saw that there were Ukrainians living there, people I hadn't known from before the war. They yelled at me to leave and never come back.

I never found out what happened to Gedalya Erlich, the man who took myself and my friend Baruch Kopyt under his wing in the Karachun forest. After liberation we lost touch. In fact, I lost touch with Baruch as well, and I never managed to meet up with him again – though not for lack of trying.

Much to my delight, I met my uncle Pesach in Bereźne. I found out he was the only family I had left. He was my father's eldest brother. During the ghetto he was sent to forced labor in Kostopil', and escaped during the uprising of the Jewish prisoners against the Germans. He hid out in a different part of the forest and when he met me in Bereźne after liberation, he kissed me and told me, "You'll be like a son to me. I'll take care of you." During the war he had given all of his belongings to one of the farmers for safekeeping. The farmer's name was Vasyl and he lived in a village named Borshchivka, not far from Bereźne on the Kostopil'-Rivne Road. Pesach said, "I'll go to Vasyl and get my clothes from him. That way we'll have clothes and food." Vasyl knew our family well; I even recall he learned a little Yiddish (which was the language of the Jews). And yet it was he who killed my uncle Pesach with an axe. When Pesach went to him, he said at first, "I don't know where the clothes are, come back tomorrow." The next day that poor fool Pesach went back with another Jew. This time, Vasyl was waiting with his brothers, and they murdered both of them with axes. Pesach was my one and only surviving family member, and now he was gone and I was alone again. This story demonstrates the sheer brutality of the Ukrainians; Vasyl had always been welcome in our home, and now he had murdered my last surviving relative. And for what? For a few articles of clothing! After it happened

I went straight to a Russian officer I knew, a Jew who served in the Soviet army who went by the name of Syomka. I told him the whole story and asked if he would accompany me with a few of his soldiers to Vasyl's house. He agreed and came along with a group of Uzbek soldiers. When we got to Vasyl's house, it turned out he had already been recruited to the military and was not home. His wife was, however, and I began screaming hysterically: "You stole from my uncle and killed him! Where are the clothes?" I started breaking open all the closets and taking whatever I could find. I found Pesach's old suit and shoes, and took a six-foot length of velvet which was very valuable. I eventually sold it and got a gold coin for it. Since Vasyl wasn't home, I went to an NKVD (Russians secret police) officer and told him that this man had murdered Uncle Pesach. I also told him he had killed partisans and various other stories which weren't necessarily true. They tracked him down at his unit in the army, tried him as a murderer and collaborator, and sent him to a Siberian labor camp – where I should hope he found his swift and just demise.

There's one more family tragedy I'd like to expand upon – the Kessler family. Tzvi Kessler was the father of the family, and he had survived the Holocaust along with his wife, his beautiful blonde daughter Manya, and his three sons. Everyone was amazed that their whole family managed to survive. Unfortunately, though, their luck soon ran out. After the area was liberated, his wife and two of his sons were murdered while they were out looking for food at a farmer's house. Not long afterward, Manya was brutally raped and murdered by Poles. Eli was the last remaining child, until he too was murdered by a Ukrainian farmer in a village named Vitkovychi. I still remember Tzvi Kessler – he was a pleasant Jew with a small mustache. One day he traveled to Warsaw and threw himself in front of a train. I suppose he committed suicide because he had lost interest in living after his entire family was wiped out…

After the death of my uncle Pesach, I was taken in by the Brayer family who had been with me in the forest.

During that time, the thing I wanted most of all was to exact revenge and fight the Germans. Every single day I went to the Russian headquarters in Bereźne and asked to enlist. Finally they took me to a high-ranking Russian officer – a lieutenant colonel. He told me, "I can't draft you now, but I can send you to a military boarding school, and they will make an officer out of you." He wrote a letter, stamped it, and sent me along with some other Jewish boys to an officers' training course at the Suvorov military boarding school in Kursk, Russia. Kursk is a very large city about 450 miles east of Bereźne. It was the scene of the most epic armored battle of World War II between the Russians and Germans, which ended with a Russian victory.

There were six of us who were sent to the boarding school – including Eli Kessler and Yosele Brayer who were both with me in the forest. During wartime, the Russians drafted all young residents in every village, town or city that they captured from the Germans. Our area was no different – all the young Ukrainians were swept up and sent to a recruitment base in Kyiv, the capital of Ukraine. The group of children that I was with tagged along with the recruits because we were traveling in the same direction. We were to get from Bereźne to the Vitkovychi train station, about five miles away, and from there to Russia. We were supervised by a Russian sergeant major. It was already dark, and the next train didn't leave until morning, so he brought us to a woman farmer's house in Vitkovychi. Attached to the house was a tavern where the Ukrainians came to drink and have a good time. The Russian soldier told her: "You are in charge of these children's lives, you had better make sure nothing happens to them!" She agreed, of course – it wasn't like she had a choice. That night the young Ukrainians came out to drink and there was a lot of commotion. We spent the night on the tavern floor, and in the morning the door burst open. A young Ukrainian, one of the party goers from the night before, was brandishing a rifle and yelled, "Damn Jews, we'll kill you all!" The woman told him, "Penes (that was his name), don't you dare touch these Jews, I am in charge of them!" But he wouldn't listen and started firing at us. I had already scouted the place during the night in case something like this happened, and had made sure that the window I was closest to could open. I was prepared… I was always alert and very resourceful by now. The Ukrainian shot at us with his rifle and killed Eli Kessler, one of the children who had been with me in the forests, but I jumped out of the window and escaped. The war was already over in the area, but those Ukrainians still had it in for us and still came after us. This was something that happened to many Jews in many different places. I immediately went to the NKVD (the Russian secret police) and told them the whole story. Penes, the Ukrainian who shot us, was caught and placed on military trial. I testified against him and he was sentenced to death. He was a Ukrainian nationalist, but I'm not sure which group he belonged to. There were two main groups of Ukrainian nationalists:

the "Banderovci" – the followers of Stepan Bandera; and the "Bulbovci" – the followers of Taras Bulba. Both of these groups fought alongside the Germans against the Russians, and it was men from these groups who joined the Ukrainian militias and participated in the mass murder of the Jews, or served as guards in the concentration camps under the SS. One of them was Ivan Demjanjuk, who was tried in Israel in 1986. Their headquarters were in the eastern Polish city of Lviv. Once the Russians had pushed the Germans back into western Poland, they turned their sights on the nationalist Ukrainians and destroyed them as well. But as long as those Ukrainians were around, Jews were still being killed – even after the war was over…

Having survived the attack in Vitkovychi, minus Eli Kessler, we made our way to the military boarding school in Kursk. On the way we traveled through Kyiv, which was completely demolished. When we got to Kursk, we were given uniforms and proudly referred to as "future officers". But the young Ukrainian gentiles mocked us, saying "How could a Jew become an officer?" At first I really wanted to become an officer, but there was no getting away from the antisemitism… We found it increasingly unpleasant and started getting homesick. Some of us still had families and we just wanted to get out of there. Several times we asked to leave, and eventually we were discharged. We took off our uniforms and put on civilian clothing. Initially we were housed in an orphanage, and from there we traveled back to Ukraine on the train, free of charge. The trains were full of soldiers and those wounded in battle or on the home front. And so it was that several months after I left, I was back in Bereźne.

# CHAPTER 5:
# WANDERING, AND A NEW HOMELAND

Upon returning to Bereźne in the fall of 1944, I was taken in by the Berman family who took care of me and treated me like a son. They were lucky enough that their entire family had survived. I lived with them in Bereźne and also helped them make a living. We would buy vodka, eggs, and butter from the farmers and sell it all in Sarny, a town about 30 miles north of Bereźne. The roads were extremely dangerous because the nationalist Ukrainian gangs still roamed the area and attacked civilians and military forces. Therefore, we traveled in Red Army trucks and were guarded by the soldiers. I remember they used to fire in the air off the back of the truck in order to test their weapons.

The Bermans had survived because they had hidden in the village of Knyazivka, not far from Bereźne. The father of the family, Felyk Berman, knew the village reverend who helped his family hide – himself, his wife Selyk and their two daughters Judith and Rachel. They basically adopted me when I got back to Bereźne from the military boarding school in Kursk. I remember they always used to give me a slice of cake on the Sabbath.

I kept in touch with the Bermans after making Aliyah (immigration) to Israel as well. They were very proud of me for serving in the military. I went to visit them several times at their home in Lod. They desperately wanted me to marry their daughter Judith. She was a good friend of mine, and I did in fact intend to marry her, but unfortunately she died of cancer at a very young age during the War of Independence (1947-1949). The family later moved to Ramat Gan and I did stay in touch with them over the years.

Under the Russians, children's studies were compulsory. And so it was that I went to a Russian school together with the Berman daughters Judith and Rachel. We were the only three Jews in the entire school, which wasn't too surprising as there were barely any Jews left. Our teacher was Lydia Gauvna, whose gravesite I noticed on our family trip to Bereźne a few years ago. She was married to a Ukrainian from Kyiv.

The Russians wanted to spread Communism in Ukraine, so they brought all sorts of engineers and officials from Kyiv, including the teacher Lydia. I was a very good student. I loved history, especially Russian history – the stories were very compelling to me. There are some Russian songs I still know how to sing. When I told Lydia I was leaving and traveling to Palestine, she said, "Why, Sucha, why are you going? Stay here and become a historian, you'll be a fine professor!" But I was steadfast and told her I was leaving.

Sadly, the vast majority of Jews who survived and came back to Bereźne looking for their homes and loved ones never found them. They did not wish to stay on Ukrainian soil, soaked with Jewish blood, and where Jews were still occasionally being murdered by the locals. Most of them wanted to immigrate to the Land of Israel. I remember one day in 1945, when the Nazis had not yet been fully defeated, the head of the local branch of the communist party gathered all the residents in the town square and gave a rousing speech: "The Red Army has liberated us from the Nazis. From now on this is our eternal homeland, and we will live here in security and in peace!" So he said, but we Jews felt entirely differently...

Perhaps 80 or 100 Jews who were originally from Bereźne or the surrounding areas gathered in the town after liberation of the area. At some point they held a memorial for the murdered next to the site of the killing pits. I remember several days earlier they had partially opened the pits to see who was buried there, and then resealed them. It was awful! The war was still ongoing, and occasionally there were funerals held at Bereźne's Christian cemetery for fallen soldiers. Out of curiosity I attended a few of them, including one for a pilot who was considered a war hero.

After the war ended, most of the Jews who had come back to Bereźne traveled west toward Germany, where most Jewish war refugees assembled at the time. Out of 3,500 Jews who had lived in Bereźne before the war, barely 100 survived. Some of them had hidden in the forests, like myself. Others had been taken in by kind-hearted gentiles, or joined the partisans. Others still managed to escape deep into Soviet territory. A very small minority of those survivors stayed in Bereźne for years after that; most of us had returned only to seek out surviving relatives – and once that hope had been extinguished, there was no reason to stay any longer. A short while after the war had ended, the Russians decided to make eastern Poland a part of Soviet Ukraine, and engaged in population replacement.

Jews and Poles from the greater Bereźne area were sent west to Poland, and were replaced by Ukrainians. And so it was that at the end of 1945, I left Bereźne with other Jews and arrived at the first stop on my journey to the Land of Israel – the Jewish orphanage in the Polish city of Bielsk. There we were received by our educator Stanislaw Pomeranz, whom I remember well.

It was at Bielsk where I first began to grow close to the United Kibbutz Movement. They sent a guide from Palestine named Mordechai Goldberg. He organized our group and several weeks later we traveled to a Displaced Persons (DP) camp in Germany. In an ironic twist of fate, our train stopped next to the Auschwitz death camp in Poland! One of the youths in our group who was a little older was a teenager named Gilinski, and he had been held at Auschwitz during the war and survived. He was tasked with shining the Germans' boots and was thus saved from gas chambers. While we were waiting for the next train, he gave us a tour of the camp, showing us the mounds of human hair, the furnaces, and the bunks in the shacks they slept in. From there we traveled to Plzeň, Czechoslovakia, and from there to Munich and Landsberg in Bavaria, southern Germany (Landsberg was where Hitler was imprisoned after a failed coup in 1923. Of course he later seized power through democratic elections…). There were several DP camps throughout Germany in those days, including in Landsberg, Aschau, Freiburg, and others. These were usually camps that were originally SS or Wehrmacht bases that had been repurposed to house us. We received aid from the International Red Cross and from American Jews. They sent us packages with clothing, food, and other assorted items. We stayed at the St. Ottilien Archabbey –

a monastery which also had a large hospital. It had previously served as a sanatorium for German officers. Finally, after years of hunger and malnutrition, we had an abundance of very fine food! As children, we were the minority among many adults, and we were looked upon favorably and treated kindly by the older people. They were genuinely impressed and delighted that there had been Jewish children who had survived the horrors.

The place had a concert hall, and I still remember the people used to gather and host singalongs. The Jewish girls and young women who had an opportunity to perform and sing would put on a show, and we would sit and take it all in.

At the DP camp, the youth were organized into several youth movements. There was Dror, Hashomer Hatzair, Gordonia, and the Religious Kibbutz movement. I was a part of Dror, which belonged to the United Kibbutz movement. Sometimes, as a group, we would march down the streets of Landsberg in front of the locals. Our counselor would lead the line, and we would sing homeland songs in Hebrew and Yiddish. One of us would beat a drum. We were good Zionists, and well organized – a bona fide youth movement! I'm sure the Germans were slightly bemused. They would stare at us silently, probably thinking, "Look at those Jews… not long ago they were being marched to their deaths and now here they are marching in our streets." They stood there without being able to do anything, because now we were strong and it was the Germans who were weak. Perhaps they also felt guilty. You could say I miss that time, the whole ambience… we were treated really well by the Germans; they were serving us! There were beautiful German women who would cook and clean and make our beds for us – and we were only about fourteen or fifteen years old. I was chosen to be in charge of supplies and food, so I gorged myself on butter and all sorts of delicious foods and put on quite a bit of weight. The German girls would hug and kiss me and I could have had a good time with them, but I was still young and so I gave them some food without any sexual favors in return.

The camps were run by the Americans and the Jewish Agency, and they made sure we were well taken care of with clothing and food. It was in those camps that the Jews began to be organized in Zionist movements in preparation for making Aliyah – immigrating to Israel (which was then still known as Palestine).

For Jews in the DP camps, there wasn't much to do during the days… we used to play soccer, biding our time and awaiting the signal to leave for Palestine. They brought in a German who taught us how to play soccer. I played the right-back position, and enjoyed the game immensely.

When we were at St. Ottilien, we were visited by a Jewish director, originally from Lithuania, who had also survived the concentration camps. He organized us on behalf of "Dror" to put on a play. The play was titled "Clippers and Iron" and I was chosen to play the lead role. I was a blacksmith, and I had an assistant named Jupiter. The play had a theme song titled *Grüne Felde, Lange Wege* ("Green Fields, Long Roads"). The play had a Zionist concept, of Jews who had survived the Holocaust and wanted to immigrate to the Promised Land but were denied entry by the British. It was in fact a politically charged ideological play. The iron is processed by the blacksmith, and the clippers are used to prune trees and bushes. This was the representation of the integration of agriculture and industry. I remember the night we put on the play, there was a group of Greek Jews who weren't allowed into the theater. They were members of the right-wing Beitar political youth movement headed by Ze'ev Jabotinsky. They were hotheaded, those Greeks, and they had knives and started brawling with the ushers. They were not fans of the concept of the play, because "Dror", a faction of the United Kibbutz movement, was aligned with more left-wing politics. The backdrop of the whole conflict between the factions was the question of how to treat the British government who allowed only a limited immigration of Holocaust survivors to Palestine. The Left supported a cooperative attitude despite it all, while the Right led an armed resistance against the Brits through its underground units Etzel – The National Military Organization and Lehi – Fighters for the Freedom of Israel. That brawl saw several young boys from Dror stabbed and wounded. It is quite astonishing that Jews who had survived the Holocaust were standing on German soil and fighting with other Jews because of political differences. It was basically a horrible war between Jews on ideological grounds. I'm sure the Germans looked on, thinking, "Look at those Jews killing each other!" I remember the incident well because it caused a great stir in the camp, and it was even the subject of an article in the local Jewish Holocaust survivors newspaper called *Unser Wort* ("Our Word").

We stayed at St. Ottilien in Landsberg for about one year, and we were then transferred to a different camp at Aschau, also not far from Munich, the capital of Bavaria. When we were there, we met an emissary from Palestine, Zivia Lubetkin, who was the wife of Yitzhak "Antek" Zuckerman – both were famous for the roles they had played in the Warsaw ghetto uprising. They later established the Israeli kibbutz of Lohamei Haghettaot ("The Ghetto Fighters") and the museum which goes by the same name, also situated on the kibbutz. Zivia came to the camp to tell us about Palestine, and we were very enthusiastic.

We were encouraged to take up writing during our stay at the DP camps. I wrote my first poem when we got to Aschau, not long after we had moved from Landsberg. It was a poem about Kibbutz Yagur. It was just after Operation Agatha, dubbed "Black Sabbath" by the Israelis, when the British laid siege to several Jewish settlements – mainly kibbutzim – and searched for weapons and made multiple arrests. They found mortars and many other weapons in Yagur, and it left quite an impression on us. I originally wrote the poem in Yiddish, because my Hebrew was still quite poor back then. The poem was later translated to Hebrew. It was a zealous poem titled "Yagur, You Have Fallen, But Again You Shall Rise". Our counsellor Mordechai Goldberg was the one who encouraged us to write. He told me I had a talent for writing. Despite my attempt at humility by saying my writing was full of mistakes, he still encouraged me to continue writing. And so I did. I would write social critiques about the other youths at the camp. It was our way of engaging in conflict with our friends – using words instead of our fists. They used to write that I was a butter aficionado (which was true), and I would retort with my own comebacks.

My writing back then was tainted with my Holocaust experience, even if it wasn't directly written about it. The trials and tribulations I had been through had affected my mood, as well as my mental and physical state. I managed to find a way to express myself through writing, and I received support from people around me. I was always proud when I completed a poem, although I must admit I did it mostly to find favor with the girls. I wasn't tall or well-built, I was a frail young boy and there was one girl who I wished to impress.

In preparation for our immigration to Palestine, the Jewish Agency conducted all sorts of medical tests. In order to be approved for immigration one had to be of a certain height, weight and physical condition – and I was weak and underweight. I didn't meet their criteria and therefore I could not go. Those of us who didn't make the cut were told, "Wait and get stronger, and then you'll be approved". I pleaded my case with them incessantly until they sent me to the Jewish Agency's clinic in Munich for further testing. Imagine me, a fourteen year old boy, traveling alone on a train to Munich with nothing but the clinic's address in my pocket! After several hours of wandering around and searching through the city of Munich, which had been battered and bruised by allied bombs, I finally found the clinic. On the way, in order to show a higher weight, I placed some rocks in the pocket of my raincoat that I had received in the packages sent to us at the DP camp by the American Jews. Luckily for me, the examination was superficial and they didn't tell me to take the coat off. Thus I met the required weight and was approved to immigrate to Palestine...

One day in the beginning of 1947, not long after that examination, we were suddenly assembled and placed on trucks in cooperation with the American military. They closed the tarps around us and told us to sit in silence. We traveled to Port de Bouc near the southern French city of Marseille. This was the first time in my life I had seen ships. I saw one big ship and inquired, "Is that going to be ours?" and was told, "Oh no, yours will be much smaller!" We stayed in Marseille for several months and lived in a big house leased by Aliyah Bet – the covert organization of the Jewish settlement in Palestine tasked with helping Jews immigrate there. There were several groups from various youth movements. We were all there together, impatiently awaiting the signal from the Aliyah Bet people to be prepared to board the ships. The Land of Israel was the foremost thing on our minds, it was all we ever talked about. We were ideologues! Finally, after waiting what seemed like an eternity, we immigrated in the winter of 1947.

The Aliyah process took place in immigration ships. Ours was nicknamed *San Miguel*, and there were 650 of us on board. They later changed its name to *Anonymous Immigrant*, after one of the immigrants who was killed in battle with the British on board the ship. There were narrow, tightly-clustered bunks with a ceiling so low you couldn't even sit on them. It was a small merchant ship converted to a passenger rig to fit as many people as possible. The ship's captain was a pleasant man named Yosele Dror of Kibbutz Maagan Michael. We would stand on the deck singing homeland songs. When we approached the shores of Palestine, the British stopped us about ten miles short of the coast. They surrounded us with four or five warships and addressed us over a loudspeaker: "You are illegals, and you may not enter." We prepared for all-out war: we gathered the canned food and bottles we had and readied ourselves to pelt the British with them. I was fully dedicated to the cause, and when they boarded our ship, I stood in front of one of the soldiers, took off my shirt and told him, "Schiss", which means "Shoot" in Yiddish. I earned my new nickname right there "Shmilke Schiss", but the soldier said, "No, baby," meaning I was just a child. Before they boarded they dispersed tear gas. The stronger youths from Dror put up a fight, pelting them with cans of food and bottles, and started a brawl. Everyone was coughing from the gas and I almost choked. Eventually they took control of the ship and forced us to sail to the port of Haifa. We decided we would go on hunger strike. Not everyone cooperated, so our counselor told me, "You're well-spoken – give one of your speeches and tell people not to eat." I stood up and gave a passionate speech laced with Zionist rhetoric. We reached Haifa port and slept overnight on the ship. In the morning they marched us between two rows of armed sailors onto the huge British ship *Ocean Wigan*, which took us to the illegal immigrants' detention camp in Cyprus. The ship sailed the Haifa-Cyprus route, regularly shuttling illegal immigrants without immigration certificates to Cyprus; and those immigrants who were in Cyprus and had been approved entry, were shuttled back. That was the first time I traveled on that ship – the second was two months later, when we returned from Cyprus to Haifa.

We reached Cyprus at dusk. We saw people milling about behind barbed wire fences, taking showers outdoors. That was the first glimpse I had of Cyprus – the heavily fenced camps eerily reminiscent of the Holocaust. There were several camps in the area, and I was assigned to camp 65. Inside the camp they housed us in little tin shacks with tin roofs, tightly arranged in rows. Above the camps there was a bridge because on the ground they were separated by walls and fencing. The atmosphere was pretty good. We were visited by emissaries from Palestine and were taught to speak Hebrew. Our group in the camp was called "Atid Revivim", named after Kibbutz Revivim in the Negev.

There wasn't much to do in Cyprus except wait. We played some soccer or watched others play, just like in the DP camps in Germany.

There was quite a bit of antagonism among the various political youth movements at the camp – Dror, Hashomer Hatzair, and Beitar. There were fights and the occasional brawl, stemming from the intense resentment and hatred between Beitar and the other youth movements. Dror and Hashomer Hatzair were affiliated with the official institutions of the Jewish settlement in Palestine, and with the Haganah – the paramilitary wing of the Jewish settlement. Beitar, on the other hand, was affiliated with the Irgun and Lehi – the underground paramilitary arms of the political right wing. Later on, Dror and Hashomer Hatzair merged and established *Mapam* – the United Workers' Party. I remember the Beitar youths always used to call us traitors and collaborators with the British. Just as it had been in Germany, the Holocaust survivors fought amongst themselves in Cyprus as well.

We stayed in Cyprus for about eight months before we were approved to immigrate to Palestine on account of us being juveniles. At first we were sent to Atlit detention camp. From there we were taken to Kibbutz G'lil Yam. I was already sixteen years old, and the Independence War had broken out. We were young, and being adventurous we wished to join the Palmach – the elite fighting force of the Jewish community during the period of the British Mandate for Palestine. We were approached by the head of "Youth Immigration" in Palestine who told us, "You're only children, you're not old enough to enlist. This will corrupt your personality, as Holocaust survivors you should build your families and not join the war." But we were steadfast and told him we nevertheless wished to be drafted. This was at the very end of 1947, just after the Independence War had started. There had just been the famous refinery massacre in which thirty-nine Jewish workers had been killed by Arab rioters at the Haifa refineries. This was what triggered my final decision to join the Palmach.

After I enlisted, they took us to Camp Yonah (Beit Lid) where we underwent training and joined Company C of the famous Palmach 4th Battalion dubbed *Haportzim*. The battalion was part of the Harel Brigade and was commanded by Dado Elazar, who later became the IDF Chief of Staff. The commander of the brigade was Yosele Tabenkin. I fought in the battles of Jerusalem and later also in the Negev as part of Operation *Horev*. The Golani brigade attacked from Rafah, while we attacked from Auja al-Hafir. My background in World War II meant I was inspired by the Red Army who had liberated us from the Nazis. During battles I would use the battle cry "Hura", which means "Forward" in Russian, as well as "Za Rodinu! Za Stalina!" which means "For the Motherland and for Stalin!".

One cold, dark night we were tasked with capturing an Egyptian post. We lay quietly waiting for the artillery barrage to cease. We were barely breathing for fear of the Egyptians hearing us. I was second machine gunner, which meant I carried the cartridges for the machine gun. By then, we were strong young men. During the battle my squad commander Ziss told me to go help machine gunner Itzik with his Bren machine gun which had jammed. We couldn't get it to work, so Ziss told me to go to the Egyptian post we had just captured and get a machine gun. I thought my end was near, but I couldn't say no... besides, I was a young and zealous fighter. I went into the outpost which had sandbag fortifications around it and stepped on an Egyptian soldier lying there. He wasn't dead, he had just passed out. I took a Bren machine gun from the outpost and brought it to Itzik. In any other army I would have gotten a medal of excellence, but Ziss just slapped me on the soldier and said, "Good job, Sucha".

We were youths who had come from the Diaspora, and as such we admired the more seasoned Palmach veterans and looked up to them. I don't remember the Holocaust survivors ever being looked down upon by the *Sabras* (Israeli natives), or treated as outsiders – but we certainly admired them. There was one girl from Kibbutz Ein Harod named Rachel Savorai. Her family was well-known and was one of the founders of the kibbutz. She fought with the Palmach, she had a rifle and she could shoot as well as any man. She was a fine soldier. There were quite a few female fighters in the Palmach, it wasn't uncommon at all. There were many good people, including in our own platoon which was comprised of Youth Society members from Kibbutz G'lil Yam. I still have photos of my fellow fighters in the Palmach.

Those who had survived the Holocaust kept saying how important it was to stay alive and build families, to make sure the chain of life was not broken... and yet, throughout the war I kept telling myself, "You stayed alive, you survived and got through everything – the Nazis, the cold winters in the forests, the Ukrainian nationalists, and everything else – and now you've come here to die in battle. There'll be nothing left of your family..." The battles were incessant and I was lucky to stay alive. It's hard to explain – on the one hand I do not believe in God; and on the other hand it feels like God was watching out for me. While I don't believe in eternal life, I believe I stayed alive because I have a duty to tell my story.

During the war, the Palmach was disbanded, and when the fighting ceased, they sent 15% of the fighters to commander or officer training. I volunteered, but they told me I didn't have to go. When the war was over they told us, "You're discharged, you don't have to continue serving in the army. Go and build a kibbutz. And so it was that we, the G'lil Yam youths of the Palmach, eventually joined the founders of *Kibbutz Mashabei Sadeh* in the Negev. This was in 1949, at a time when there were many settlements and kibbutzim cropping up all around the country, including those founded by members of youth movements who had served in the Palmach.

I was called up for reserve duty in the southern brigade for Operation Kadesh (the Sinai Campaign) in 1956, but never saw battle. By the outbreak of the Six Day War in 1967, I was already in Kibbutz Shamir. I was part of the regional defense forces tasked with guarding the kibbutz. All the kibbutz members who were reservists in the IDF and weren't enlisted in the combat units were summoned for training and undertook guard duty.

During the Yom Kippur war in 1973 I was still part of the Shamir regional defense. Several years later I was permanently discharged from reserve duty.

# CHAPTER 6:
# FAMILY, WORK AND REMEMBRANCE

Along with several of my fellow Palmach fighters, I arrived at Kibbutz Mashabei Sadeh in 1949, at the end of the War of Independence. During the first few years, I worked at the bakery. I would bake the dough for bread, challah, cakes and so on... Then in 1952, I became a counselor at *Hanoar Haoved Vehalomed* (Working and Studying Youth movement), which was affiliated with the United Kibbutz movement. At first I was the coordinator for the Lod chapter, and later I moved to Givatayim and served as counselor for the Bnei Brak chapter. Then in 1955, the kibbutz sent me to "Efal Seminar" for six months, at Ramat Efal near Tel Aviv. It was an ideological seminar run by the kibbutz movement. We studied Zionism, Israeli studies, Jewish history and more. I was one of the youngest students there and everyone loved me. Aside from elementary school in Bereźne, this would be the only time I ever studied in a formal setting. In 1956, I was hospitalized for almost a year in "Meir" hospital in Kfar Sava, due to the tuberculosis which I most probably caught during the Holocaust. There were many survivors who caught it during the war, and in some cases it manifested many years later. After being discharged, my love of writing led me to journalism. I served as a reporter and deputy editor for *Bama'ale*, the periodical of Hanoar Haoved Vehalomed, until I moved to Kibbutz Shamir in 1960.

I first met my wife Bracha while I served as coordinator of the youth movement chapter in Lod. At the time, she was a counselor for "Hashomer Hatzair" in Ramle. This was during a period of protests against then US Secretary of State John Foster Dulles, due to the Americans' cold attitude towards Zionism. The youth movements in our area organized a protest against him, and that is where we met. This was sometime during 1953 or 1954. Bracha was a member of Kibbutz Shamir. She had grown up in Kibbutz Ein HaHoresh along with a group of immigrants from her native Romania, which later moved to Shamir. Most of them had left by then, but Bracha stayed. For a variety of reasons, we decided to live on a kibbutz. Bracha was a "diehard fan" of Kibbutz Shamir. We got married in 1959, lived for a year in Mashabei Sadeh, and then moved to Shamir in 1960.

When we first came to Shamir, I worked as a cobbler. I had studied cobbling under Ben Zion Salmanovich. There were two other workers from Kiryat Shmona working with me. Cobbling is a noble profession. It is known that the great Jewish scholar Shimon bar Yochai (The Rashbi) was also a cobbler. Later I worked for several years in the apple orchards. I was one of the quicker apple pickers around! I worked with groups of tourist volunteers from abroad, who used to stay for short periods at the various kibbutzim and help with the field work.

In the late 1960s, both prior to and after the Six Day War, I worked as a journalist. Under kibbutz terminology, my title was known as an "enlisted emissary". I was a reporter for the *Itim* news agency, as well as for Al *Hamishmar*, the newspaper of Hashomer Hatzair. I wrote the main page article!

I never went to any school or university, but I had the talent for writing – so I just wrote, off the top of my head. I am basically self-taught; almost everything I know I picked up by myself. I wrote a great deal, and it was usually interesting. For example, just before the Six Day War (1967) I wrote about a Syrian plane that was downed near Lake Kinneret. I crossed the Kinneret lake by boat and traveled to Kibbutz Ein Gev, where I wrote the story of the downed plane. I also wrote about the fledgling Kibbutz Snir which was established immediately following the war. When two infiltrators were killed near Kibbutz Maayan Baruch, I photographed them and wrote about the incident. I would never drive, and I didn't have a car. I would commission a car and a driver from the kibbutz, or else I would ride along with my fellow journalist Danny Zidkoni. Occasionally, I would call a cab from Kiryat Shmona or even hitchhike. There were also some risky ventures. Prior to the Six Day War, Kibbutz Gadot, about 13 miles south of Shamir, was shelled. I traveled there to conduct several interviews. My wife Bracha was afraid I might get killed, but I kept at it.

In 1973 – just before the end of my stint as a journalist – David Ben Horin, the kibbutz coordinator, came to me and asked if I would take over the petting zoo, which I duly accepted. On June 13, 1974, four Palestinian terrorists infiltrated Shamir from Lebanon and murdered three women. The terrorists were later killed in a firefight with kibbutz members. That morning I was taking driving lessons far in Tiberias, and was not at work. On the bus ride back, I heard there had been a terror attack in Shamir. I had been lucky not to be at work that day, as the terrorists had gone past the petting zoo at around eight o'clock in the morning, when I was usually there. I'm sure they would have killed me if I had run into them. And so once again, I escaped death! The incident only served to reinforce my belief that I was indestructible after having survived the Holocaust, the Ukrainian persecution that followed it, and the War of Independence. I worked at the petting zoo until I retired. Part of the job was also janitor work for the children's homes.[5] It was always nice to care for the animals and guide the children, both of which I am fond of. The children would come every day to work, feed the animals and milk the sheep.

Besides my job, I did other things on the kibbutz as well. For example, I put my acting talents to good use at the annual Hanukkah play "Hannah Zelda". I played Rabbi Kalman, while Sarah Gottlieb, a fellow kibbutz member, played the title role "Hannah Zelda". I also was part of the theater club and studied drama in Kiryat Shmona under the great director Nola Chelton. I also acted in several plays put on by the North Galilee regional theater club.

On top of that, I was also an amateur photographer. I used to take photos and occasionally sell them for 25 shekels apiece. It was a small side business. Photography was a hobby I used to indulge in quite often, although I no longer do.

These days, I do other things. I like to collect glass bottles: twice a day, morning and evening. I take my mobility scooter around the kibbutz grounds and collect whatever bottles I can find. I get 30 *agorot* (cents) for every bottle, so when I've

---

5. In many kibbutzim at the time, children lived communally and separately from their parents.

collected 1,500 bottles, I give them to my son Natan who takes them to Kiryat Shmona and gets 450 shekels in return. I then give the money to my grandchildren, and start collecting again. That's another one of my hobbies, I do it every day – rain or shine.

I walk about two miles on my treadmill each day, listen to the radio – mostly the news – and read the newspaper. I particularly enjoy the sports section. I mainly follow soccer, particularly the Hapoel Tel Aviv club. I always reach for the sports section first and scour the pages to see if they've written anything about them. In 1947, while I was staying at kibbutz Glil Yam, I remember I first saw them play against Herzliya, and I've been a fan ever since. They always had a respectable fanbase in Kibbuts Shamir, despite not being a local club. I first started enjoying soccer when I was in the displaced persons camps in Germany and then in the detention camp in Cyprus. There wasn't much else to do but watch the games organized by the youth movements.

I also like to pickle cucumbers, which my family loves. I leave the jars to pickle outside my house, and my children and grandchildren take them when they leave after a visit, sometimes even before they've had a chance to properly pickle. My affinity for pickled foods is something I got from my parents and grandparents. My mother and grandmother used to pickle cucumbers in a little vat and leave it out on the porch. It's a whole culture I inherited from them. The Ukrainians would pickle many vegetables; cabbage was a big favorite. While I was hiding in the forests during the war, we would steal onions and garlic from the farmers, and so I developed a liking for spicy and sour foods.

I also take care of my wife Bracha, who is currently ill, and continue to write poetry. But the most important thing, and that which I am most proud of, is my family.

**Livia**, our eldest daughter, was born in late 1959 and was four months old when we came to Shamir in 1960. We rode from Mashabei Sadeh in the local council's truck; Bracha sat next to the driver while I sat on the roof, guarding our belongings.

Livia is named after Bracha's mother, but it also has a biblical meaning – a crown of flowers that Jewish girls used to wear on their heads on *Tu Be'Av*, the Jewish equivalent of Valentine's Day.

**Natan**, our second child, was born in Shamir in 1964, and is named after my father.

**Yotam**, our youngest son, was born in 1967, during the Six Day War. We were in our shelter and wanted to come up with a name that had some military context to it. On the radio we had heard of an Israeli Air Force officer who had served in the anti-aircraft unit and shot down a Syrian plane. His name was given as "Lt. Yotam", and so we named our son after him. I am also thankful for my grandchildren and great-grandchildren.

When my children were little, I used to make up nice little stories to tell them. Conversely, I also told them about the Holocaust. My children are steeped with many memories of the Holocaust because I told them many stories. I told them often, but what I have told them is but the tip of the iceberg of what I actually endured. It's always been important to me to instill the memory of the Holocaust in my children and indeed in anyone who wishes to hear the story. However, up until recently, I had never given much thought to the impact my stories would have had on other people, my own family included.

I was always invited to come and speak and tell my story, and I always did because I knew how to tell it and I wanted to. In the beginning, I used to go to the children's' schools in the kibbutz and tell the class my story of how we would gather food in the forest and steal food from the local farmers. During the years I've been to kindergartens and schools and universities, and many other places. Some of the places I've been to more than once. Not all Holocaust survivors could summon the strength to relive these stories again and again, but I could and so I did. I did it because it's the right thing to do, and so I could leave something substantial behind when I'm gone.

The Jews had a motto in the Holocaust: "Live to Tell the Tale". There was a burning desire to stay alive for future generations. People fought like lions to stay alive. Even people who had lost their entire families still kept on fighting to live another day, in the hopes of surviving, living, and telling the story. This is why I wrote my poems and novels, and this is why I go to schools and other places and tell my story. I have told it so many times that even I have grown tired of it – telling the same thing over and over gets tedious.

Unlike me, my wife Bracha doesn't much like to talk about the Holocaust. Her family was from southern Romania. Jews in that area fared better than the Jews in Ukraine, where I am from. The Romanians had an autonomous government which collaborated fully with the Germans, and fought alongside them against the Russians. The Romanian government decided that the Jews in the south were to be spared, unlike in the northern part of the country where the Jews were massacred just like in the rest of Europe.

# CHAPTER 7:
# CREATION AND EXPRESSION

I wrote my first poems about the Holocaust on little scraps of paper while I worked at the petting zoo. I have always written on random scraps of paper. Even these days, if the mood strikes me, I take out a piece of paper and jot down my thoughts. During my stay at the DP camps in Germany before coming to Palestine, we would write what were called "creative critiques" in the form of a story or a poem. We would sit with our counselor Misha Rabinowitz, and take it in turns to read our work and listen to the others. At first I wrote in Yiddish because I didn't know any Hebrew. Then one day I took a chance and wrote something in Hebrew, which was full of mistakes. It was the first time I had written in Hebrew and I had done it to impress Sonya, a girl I was interested in. It was the first time I was in love, and I was proud of my work despite the errors. That is where I first discovered my affinity and talent for writing, and it grew from there.

Later on, I wrote humoristic critiques known as feuilletons. I started while still living in Mashabei Sadeh and continued even after we moved to Shamir. This was before I started writing poetry. When I served as editor of the Shamir newspaper for two years, I published one of my feuilletons in every newspaper. I contemplated publishing a book with a collection of feuilletons, but ultimately their popularity declined and I started writing poems. I always told myself that after I'm gone, at least there'll be something to read that was written by my own hand.

Throughout the years I wrote a great deal, but never about the topic closest to my heart – the Holocaust. I wrote a few poems but never dared publish them. My first published poem was written in memory of Avi Rotem, a member of my kibbutz who was killed in Sinai during the War of Attrition in 1969. He served as an officer, and I met him the day he left the kibbutz for the last time, a week before he fell. We spoke briefly and I remember being impressed that he took the time to converse with an elderly immigrant kibbutz member. Back then I still had an inferiority complex with regards to my relationship with native Israelis. The day they announced on the kibbutz that he had been killed, I was shaken to my core. I wrote a poem dedicated to his memory titled "Here Yesterday, Gone Today" and published it in the kibbutz newspaper.

I then summoned up the courage to go to the editor of "Poalim Library", Azriel Ukhmani of Kibbutz Ein Shemer, with a collection of my poems. He himself was a poet, and was considered the highest authority among kibbutz poets. He read my poems and exclaimed, "Where have you been hiding? You write poems! Poems worthy of seeing the light of day!" He pushed me to publish them and so I did. The first poem in the first book I published was titled "Even in Truth, We Lied to Ourselves". The book itself which was published in 1976 titled "Uttering Words Which Died in You". I wrote nine more books after that. I never believed I would write book after book, but in total, I wrote ten books: nine poem collections and one novel. Only God knows their true value... although there was one woman, a professor from Kibbutz Ein HaHoresh, who taught some of my poems, which was a great honor. Recently, I received a call from Dr. Eran Tzelgov, head of the literature department at Beersheba's Ben Gurion University. He told me he likes my poems and he teaches them at the university. Isn't that something?

I lived to tell my story of the Holocaust, but I started writing and telling at around the age of forty-five. My wife Bracha knew I had written stories and poems and encouraged me to publish them, because she thought it would help me be more like other people who had written about the Holocaust. It is much to her credit that I summoned the courage to publish my books. I used to seek her advice on certain words or phrases or stories because I trusted her instincts.

After my success writing poetry, I took the next step and wrote a novel about the Holocaust. So I wrote the autobiographical novel "A Fragment from the Planet of Ashes". And yet, any stories I tell of the Holocaust would be nothing. Anything I write or say would be merely the tip of the iceberg of what really happened.

These days I have a touch of "writer's mania" and I write an awful lot. I want to publish another book of poems, but I want it to be of higher quality. A Jew my age should write with class! The poems should be profoundly expressive. I don't know why I got the writing bug. Sometimes I can't express one word, but now I'm in sort of a "late bloomer" phase of intensive writing. Writing is hard, and I always use a pencil. I write a poem and put it in a drawer and then come back to it a month later. I look at it with fresh eyes, make corrections and put it back. And so on and so forth. I repeat the process three or four times and then look at the finished product. If it's no good, I archive it. If I like it, I'll take it to someone I can consult with and decide whether to include it in the book. I already have 300 new poems for my next book!

The great poet C.N. Bialik once said that each poet has but one poem. Each poet writes the same poem over and over, in many different versions. I write about the sky and the trees, and feelings toward my family, and emotions of love and disappointment and despair, and hope and loneliness, about my mother and my sister. All my books are written this way. They're always about the Holocaust, but what I tell is but a small part of the real story…

I've written ten books and dedicated them to my parents and my sister. A Holocaust survivor who never went to school has published ten books! My poems are taught in higher learning institutions, and my books are stocked in libraries. All this means that they have actual literary value. If I ever stopped writing, I think I would die. It's what I live for. I'm preparing to publish my eleventh book. The process of writing a book is similar to a pregnancy. The book is first conceived within you, and the writing process culminates in the labor pains of finishing the book and publishing it – the birth of a new creation. And even after it is born, you never stop thinking about it and marveling at it.

As time passes, I find myself reliving the memory of the Holocaust more and more, which is a terrible thing. Every night before I go to bed I remember all the Jews that were murdered.

I think of the little children thrown alive into the pits where they suffocated to death. I think of my own family and all the other Jews who were made to lie down in the pits before being shot by the Ukrainian militias who were only too happy to do the Germans' bidding. The Holocaust is a great lake of Jewish blood. Anything I can extract from there and pass on would be but a drop in the ocean. Six million Jews, that's about 23 million gallons of blood! Those who waded through the ocean and survived were few and far between. A person who escapes that ocean of blood can't tell you much. And what I went through is difficult to describe. An eleven-year-old boy, alone in the world, hanging on for dear life in a hostile environment where anyone could kill him at any moment. A boy battling hunger, cold, and blood-sucking lice. Try to imagine just one night where your body turns blue from cold and you warm yourself under tree branches. Even if you tried to express it in words, those words would be the wrong ones. The gist of it can be conveyed using speech or writing, but the actual reality doesn't translate on paper. I lived to tell the tale, and that's all we survivors can do, and yet the full picture, the actual enormity of the reality, remains ever elusive. This is why I still have a hunger to write and tell my stories. I continue to write, with the everlasting hope that I might be able one day to fully express the true scope of what I went through.

# CHAPTER 8:
# THE AMAZING STORY OF DASHA AND YOTAM

One of the things I'm most happy about is the fact that my wife Bracha and I have managed to make three separate trips to Ukraine, organized by the Bereźne survivors. The first trip was with Natan and Yotam, my two sons, in 2002. The next time was with Livia and Guy, my daughter and grandson, in 2005. The third time was with Adi and Nitzan, two of my granddaughters, in 2008. They were true heritage trips, and we gained some closure...

I had always wanted to go back to Volyn and Bereźne. I had wanted to visit the graves of my family and all the other Jews, but the Iron Curtain between western Europe and Soviet-controlled eastern Europe meant Israelis couldn't travel there. Only in the early 1990s, once the Soviet Union was dissolved and Ukraine became a sovereign nation, did it become possible. I have always felt a restless and extraordinary attraction to the green forests. It is truly evergreen, not like what we have in Israel. It's as if the very soil is pulling me towards it. My roots are in Bereźne. I was forcefully uprooted from it, and I still miss it.

In contrast with other Holocaust survivors who may find it difficult to return to their hometowns and relive the horrifying memories, I had no difficulty going back. I wanted very much to go, and would have gone for a fourth trip if Bracha was healthy.

It was important to me that our children and grandchildren joined us on the trip. I hope to travel one day with my great-grandchildren as well... it is very important to me that they preserve the memory of what happened, and memorialize my own murdered family. The greatest danger is forgetting! The worst death is the death of memory. The torch must be passed on to children and grandchildren so that the memories are never lost. This is why my need to pass on the memories trumps all else.

The Association of Wolynian Jews in Israel was in charge of organizing the trips we went on. The members of the association meet once a year at "Beit Volyn" in Givatayim. Beit Volyn is the memorial center of Volyn Jewry. I've been there several times, and once they even invited me to read some of my poems. Nowadays, there are very few Bereznean or Volynian Jews still alive, but those who are still hold the annual meetings.

When I got to Bereźne, the first thing I did was to go and look for my house, but I couldn't find it. The locals rebuilt many of the old houses. In Kurhany, however, I did find the house which had belonged to Soltus, the farmer I had stayed with prior to the killings. I took a photo with his daughter Nadya, who is my age and was still alive. I also gave her some local currency. She still lives in the same house she lived in all those years ago! They may have built some additions on to it, but it mostly stayed the way I remembered it. The house is right at the edge of the village, so we didn't venture into the village itself.

In Bereźne, there are two tombstones right near the three death pits, outside the Jewish cemetery. The first was erected by the city authorities during the Communists' rule. They were aware of the atrocities that had occurred there and decided to put up a tombstone. The inscription is all in Russian and it doesn't mention the Jews at all – the Communists played down any mention of religion or nationality, and only memorialized the "citizens of the USSR". The inscription states that in this place lie 3,680 citizens of the Soviet Union who were murdered and buried alive by the fascist Germans. In July 2005, following an initiative by the Association of Wolynian Jews in Israel in collaboration with the mayor of Bereźne, a second tombstone was established near the site of the first one. We participated in the unveiling during our visit that year. The new tombstone has an engraving of a menorah and reads in Hebrew: "In memory of the 3,680 martyrs of Greater Bereźne, murdered and buried alive by the cursed Nazis and their collaborators, August 25, 1942." Underneath that is a verse from an Alterman poem which reads, "And our blood in small vases you collected, because no one else would, only you alone." And right at the bottom another inscription reads, "The blood of our brothers cries out from this earth. May their souls be bound in the bond of life." The Jewish cemetery itself no longer exists. It was completely demolished and flattened. There is nothing on the site other than the signs and the memorial tombstone. The Ukrainians took all the tombstones, smashed them, and used them to pave roads and sidewalks. Occasionally I would see Hebrew letters randomly scattered along the sidewalks. At the unveiling ceremony, I gave a speech and said that the memory of the atrocities must be passed on.

One of the most amazing and happy stories that happened on our trips to Bereźne was the first time Dasha and Yotam met. Dasha is originally from the village of Stepan', about 25 miles northwest of Bereźne. The Horyn River winds through the village, and Dasha lived right by the river. Some of the residents even bathe there. Her family is a good Ukrainian family. Her grandfather, Pylyp Shyrko, was acknowledged as a Righteous Gentile and is memorialized at Yad Vashem. During the war, he hid a Jewish woman and her two sons in his house. The family survived the Holocaust and later immigrated to the United States. The woman went to Yad Vashem herself and fought tooth and nail for him to become recognized as a Righteous Gentile. On our first trip to Bereźne in 2002, myself, Bracha, Natan, and Yotam joined a dear old Jew named Yonah Keller who was with me in the forests during the war (he has since passed away). We went to visit L'ubov Shyrko, Pylyp's daughter and Dasha's aunt. That was where we first met Dasha. The aunt lives in Rivne, the largest city in the county, about 35 miles from Bereźne. Even though she is not wealthy, she served us a luxurious meal. That was where Yotam first met Dasha. We noticed a slim young woman wearing a dress and sitting off to the side. She was silent the whole time. She was staying at her aunt's at the time because she was studying engineering in Rivne. When we walked outside after finishing the meal, she accompanied us and said "Shalom", and Yotam gave her a little kiss. It reminded me of the biblical story of Jacob who kissed Rachel by the well. I was immediately taken with Dasha, and it occurred to me that she might be a good fit for Yotam. When I spoke with him about her, it turned out that he felt the same way. I asked Yonah, who spoke Ukrainian, to speak with her family on the phone and see whether they would be interested in pursuing a relationship, and wouldn't you know it – Dasha said yes!

We continued our trip, and when we got back to Israel, they started corresponding. Dasha would write in Russian, and I would take the letters to the optics factory on the kibbutz where the workers knew Russian well. They would translate to Hebrew, and we would write a letter in Hebrew which they would then translate to Russian, and we would send a letter back. I still have a stack of the letters they had written to each other. Then she came to visit him here in Israel, but she was only allowed to stay here for three months. I even went to the Interior Ministry branch in Safed to inquire about an extension, but they said she couldn't stay longer on a tourist visa. So she went back to Ukraine and they kept writing each other letters. They loved each other very much and decided to get married. Because she couldn't come here, they were officially married in Yugoslavia, where a couple can get married by way of a notary when only one side is present – Dasha was there but Yotam was not. Then Bracha and I took the marriage certificate to the Interior Ministry in Safed and Dasha was granted approval to come to Israel. We paid a lawyer quite a bit of money to help us with all the paperwork. And so Dasha came to Israel and they built a family. Eventually she also converted to Judaism, as it was important to Yotam that his wife be Jewish (according to Jewish custom, a child can be considered Jewish only if his mother is also Jewish).

Yotam and Dasha have four wonderful children. They live in Tiberias and visit us twice a week with the whole family. Dasha is extremely knowledgeable and works as a city planning engineer. She has a degree from Rivne University. She's a religious Jew now, a true gift to the Jewish nation, even if she is only one person!

Dasha's parents are good, honest Ukrainians. They accepted Dasha's marriage, her move to Israel, and her conversion quite naturally. We visited them in Stepan' on our second trip to Bereźne in 2005, and they visited us in Israel several years ago. We visited Jerusalem's churches in the Old City, as well as various other places. Dasha has two sisters who both have children. One of them is a nurse and the other works at a bank. All of her family members are high character people. They're happy for Dasha and the life she's built here, because they believe the Jewish nation to be special; they also believe she's better off here because Ukraine is nowadays quite a poor country.[6]

---

6. I think this is an amazing story! The Holocaust, with all the atrocities and horrifying stories, has also led to some incredibly unbelievable stories which far exceed one's wildest imagination. Dasha and Yotam's story fits this category nicely. It is a truly wonderful story, which in a way allows us to find a ray of light in the otherwise ghastly darkness of the Holocaust.

# CHAPTER 9:
# THE MORAL DILEMMAS OF THE HOLOCAUST

*Chapters 9 and 10 feature my conversations with Shmuel in the original question-and-answer format, rather than in the story format used in previous chapters.

**Author's questions are in bold typeface.**

**As you know, my doctoral thesis was written about the moral dilemmas Jews faced both during and after the Holocaust. It is an important topic which has not been discussed as often as one might think. There were many such dilemmas, and as part of my research I examined the opinions of Israeli youths on some of these dilemmas. You experienced the Holocaust firsthand, and possess a uniquely interesting philosophical outlook. I'd like to discuss some of these dilemmas with you and hear your opinions.**

If I know the answers I'll gladly provide them.

**In my thesis I coined the phrase "Survivalistic Morals", meaning morals which are forced upon a person who is under threat of death. This is in contrast to "Normative Morals", which are based on widely accepted laws and values followed by honest people in their day-to-day lives. Do you think that during the Holocaust it was correct to stick to widely accepted**

**moral behavior, or rather to adopt the "survivalistic" morals which inherently run counter to normative morals?**

In the Holocaust, one was forced to focus on daily survival, and therefore there was no room to even consider normative morals.

**Generally speaking, did you face any moral dilemmas during the Holocaust?**

Not at all. Look, what dictated life during those times was survival, and nothing else. It was something visceral, an indescribable internal force, something subconscious which led one to focus on surviving at all costs. This was the force that dominated existence, and provided tools for our survival. I'm talking about stealing clothes and food from the locals, all of which would be considered highly immoral under any normal circumstances. But that was what gave us the strength to live another day. Your body doesn't want to die; if we hadn't done those things we would not have survived, plain and simple. Therefore, anything considered "moral" during those times was barely relevant anymore. It's hard to explain. Your feet want to walk, your hands want to touch things. It's life, and you don't want to lose out on it. Especially in the face of the fact of so many people close to us losing their lives, we were determined to survive and live on.

I'll tell you a story to illustrate my point. I think I mentioned earlier that I had met a woman named Tony Gunar. She was only 35 years old and had five children. On the day of the mass killings at Bereźne, instead of going on the death march with everyone else, she decided to try and hide at home with her children behind stacks of firewood. She held the smallest child,

Hershele, close to her chest. From their hiding place, she heard how the Ukrainians broke into the house and rounded up the children one by one, raping her eldest daughter as well. When they were done, they took them all to the death pits. She lay there quietly with Hershele, until they had left; miraculously they had not been discovered. At night she left with him and arrived at the same place I was hiding – the barn behind Henrik the farmer's house. I lay there sleeping among the haystacks and in the morning they were there alongside me. I was not aware of her story at the time, and when she saw me acting like a normal, happy child, she scratched my face so deeply I still have the scar. She exclaimed, "All the Jews are dead and you're laughing?"

The point of the story is that she told me, "I stayed alive only for Hershele, so that he could stay alive too." And yet later he was also murdered by Ukrainian farmers when he was out looking for food. And despite it all, Tony went on living. She came to Israel and went on with her life. I even visited her with Bracha at her home in Kibbutz Givat Haim. Hershele had been all she had left in the world. And in his own bid for survival he went out looking for food, and the farmers he went to get it from caught him and killed him. And this woman, though she remained utterly alone and broken, still fought on. Even though she had told me that if Hershele were ever to die, she would just go and turn herself over to the Germans, she never did. She survived and came to Israel and remarried, although she never had any more children. I remember one year she was given the honor of lighting the candles at the memorial on Holocaust Day at the Association of Wolynian Jews in Israel.

Ultimately, despite the bottomless grief and sorrow and loss, humans still inherently wish to live on. This is one small story which illustrates that truth. She remained all alone and yet continued to fight. I wrote a poem about her titled "Tony and her five children". She passed away not long ago.

Another cruel truth is that the instinct of an individual is to protect one's own life first. Under threat of death, there were mothers who, in order to keep their young ones quiet, covered their mouths so tightly that they suffocated. This means that the mother's own life means more to her than her child's. People may say what they like, but in such a cruel reality a person is a slave to his or her own survival. There were many such stories. It contrasts with the biblical story of Hannah and her seven children during the time of the Maccabees, where she decided that she would die along with them in order not to desecrate God's name. The primal human mechanism dictates that a person fights to survive at all times, in order to preserve his destiny to live. After the Holocaust, there were some people who went and bought nice leather boots, fancy suits, and pursued money and women, despite their whole family being wiped out just years prior. How can you explain that? I saw Jews in Munich after the Holocaust who didn't join Zionist movements or immigrate to Israel. They stayed in Germany and made a lot of money. They became wealthy and established business empires, and left their riches for their children, who also still live in Germany. At most, they come to visit Israel very occasionally. These are Holocaust survivors just like I am. Their entire families were wiped out by the Nazis, and yet after the war they went to the very country the Nazis came from and made their fortunes. It's very hard to understand.

Now I'll present seven moral dilemmas which were relevant during the Holocaust and which I covered in my thesis.

The first dilemma is called the "Judenrat" dilemma. The Judenrat was the Jewish council that ran the ghettos under German orders. At some point, the Germans told the Judenrat to compile lists of Jews based on daily quotas, ostensibly to be sent to forced labor in the east. However, they understood that these were in fact lists of people who were to be sent to their deaths. The dilemma is, what should the head of the Judenrat do in such a case? Should he compile the lists and send the Jewish Police to round the Jews up or should he defy the orders?

It's hard for me to say. We had a Judenrat in Bereźne but it was on a smaller scale. Jews were sent from the ghetto to forced labor in Kostopil'. The Judenrat would send 400 or 500 Jews to work each day. I didn't work because I was still too young. The Jews who were sent to work were given 250 grams of food a day, which was 50 grams more than those who didn't work. The German method was to exhaust the Jews, strip them of their possessions and dignity, and eventually lead them like lambs to the slaughter, if they weren't already dead by then. The Germans did whatever they pleased, including using Jews to murder other Jews. These were the Judenrat, they were mere figureheads, because it was the Germans who controlled them as if by remote control.

**Did the heads of the Judenrat in Bereźne think that the Jews they sent to work were in danger of death?**

I assume they knew. The head of the Jewish Police, affiliated with the Judenrat, was Meir Keller. He was a powerful man who was appointed the head of the police. The policemen wore white armbands with a Star of David. I still remember their faces to this day. During the period before the killings, the Germans wanted to humiliate and derive whatever utility they could out of the Jews. Then they placed them in ghettos, tortured them, and eventually killed them. The Jews were killed by the Germans and their local collaborators, but it was other Jews who enforced the German rule in the ghetto up to that point. The Judenrat thought that they would be saved if they worked for the Germans. At first this was true; their status was superior to the rest of the Jews. But eventually Meir Keller and his family were also killed. Everyone was murdered on that summer's day at the death pits.

**The next dilemma is called the "Little Smuggler" dilemma. In the ghettos there were many children who ventured out to smuggle food into the ghetto. Those who were caught were usually killed. You were also a child during those times. The dilemma parents faced was whether to endanger the lives of their children and send them to procure food from outside the ghetto walls.**

The children in the ghettos ventured out to find food in order to care for their siblings and their families. In many cases their parents were already dead. This was not your normal everyday human life. These children were so thin and wispy. They wore old rags in which they managed to hide a few beets or carrots. They were starving. It was natural to do what they did. If they hadn't done it many of them wouldn't have survived. The parents also didn't have much of a choice; it was the only way for them to obtain enough food to somehow go on living. Only children were small enough to fit through the narrow openings in the ghetto walls and fences.

**The next dilemma involves parents sending away their children. There were many Jewish parents who sent their children to churches, monasteries or local residents – usually people they knew – so that the children would be raised as Christians and be saved from their fate. The dilemma for those parents was whether to part with their children perhaps forever – and send them to an unknown fate?**

I'm not aware of many such cases in Bereźne, but I was of course sent by my parents to Soltus the Ukrainian farmer, so in effect I am one of those children. It proved to be my lease of life, and I believe that the parents who sent their children away did the right thing.

**The next dilemma is known as the "Rebels' Dilemma". There were several ghettos and camps in which the Jews decided to take up arms and rebel against the Germans even though they knew that by doing so they were risking the lives of the majority who chose not to participate in the uprising. It was well known that the Germans would kill many people for even the slightest act of resistance. Should they have rebelled or not?**

The point at which these uprisings happened was usually at a time when the Germans were already preparing to kill all the Jews, such as at the labor camp at Kostopil' near Bereźne. The reason these uprisings didn't occur earlier was because they hoped the war would end and they would be saved. I believe that to be the case at the most famous ghetto of them all – the Warsaw ghetto. At the time of the Bereźne killings, there was one man who cried out for everyone to run for their lives, and attempted to escape. There were others who tried to escape as well but they were cut down immediately.

**The next dilemma is called the "Thieves' Dilemma". At the labor camps and the death camps there were many cases of prisoners stealing food from other prisoners. Should they have done that or not?**

Whether a person is good or bad is a matter of his own choice. Sometimes, however, even a good man does bad things which run counter to his own values and conscience. These were such cases in my view. They knew that what they were doing was morally wrong, but they did it out of a necessity to survive because they were starving.

**The next dilemma is known as the "Crying Baby Dilemma". The Germans searched incessantly for Jews hiding in attics or basements. Many times when they were closing in on Jews' hiding places, babies would start crying and in an attempt to silence them, the parents would cover their mouths to avoid their hiding place being discovered. There were multiple cases which ended with the baby dying. Should the parents have done so?**

You can never judge a person with the sword of death hanging over his head. There are people who would say, "Even if I were to die I wouldn't do it", but in reality there are very few people who would follow through on that. A mother knows that if the baby keeps on crying, the Nazis would find them and kill them all anyway, so she does the only possible thing that would somehow keep her alive and smothers the baby. She would never want to do it for all the riches in the world, but the fear of death trumps all else.

**The final dilemma is called the "Sonderkommando Dilemma". These were Jewish prisoners who were forcibly employed at the gas chambers and furnaces in the death camps. Should they have agreed to do so and thereby be an accessory to the killings, or should they have resisted under threat of sure death?**

The death camps had special units of Jewish prisoners who did the Germans' dirty work for them. They removed their fellow prisoners' clothing, collected the bodies and burned them in the furnaces, collected all the personal items and clothing that was left, etc. The Zyklon B gas was administered by the Germans, but the Jews did everything else. They were forced to do so; if they had disobeyed, they would have been killed anyway, so what was the point of resisting? Ultimately they were also murdered, and only a few of them survived.

**I will now move on to the dilemmas facing the Jews after the Holocaust.**

**The first one is titled "The Avengers' Dilemma". It deals with the question of retribution vs. fair trial. After the Holocaust there were Jews who independently hunted down and killed Nazi war criminals, whether alone or in organized groups.**

**Was it morally right to summarily execute Nazis without them being prosecuted in a court of law? After all, mistaken identity could lead to innocent people being killed.** There were of course many Jews who wanted revenge and killed Germans. There was a grouped named "Nakam" (Revenge), organized and led by Abba Kovner, a writer who was also a Holocaust survivor. They also had a plan to poison the water in certain German cities so as to kill millions of Germans. These were childish and impulsive plans, and couldn't have been accomplished by a small group of Jews. If after the war, the victorious Allies had decided to punish the German people by bombing them, poisoning their water, denying them food and destroying them, it could have been done. Morally speaking, there was room to consider it. It was certainly possible – the USA, England, and the USSR controlled Germany, which was completely hopeless and defeated. But the Germans are a nation of 80 million people, who by and large were being exonerated in the immediate aftermath of the war. I was in Germany when I stayed at the DP camps and witnessed the locals cowering and being afraid of everything. They worked for us when we lived in the children's quarters. There were German women who cleaned and made our beds, did our laundry and cooked for us… they were humiliated then, but look at them now, they're one of the prominent nations in Europe.

Here's a story about retribution: After the war, a year or two after liberation, I was staying at the DP camp near Munich. I was on a train and saw a man who was the spitting image of Alfred Klanz, the Nazi commander who had been in charge of the Bereźne area. He was a monster of a man and everyone had been terrified of him. As a boy, I had always entertained the notion of getting to kill him one day. I had a pocketknife with me, and the whole way I considered jumping him and stabbing him to death, but I was too scared and I wasn't totally convinced it was really him. Eventually, I said loudly, "Klanz, Klanz," figuring that if he turned and faced me, I would know it was him and I would start hollering for the other passengers to catch him. The train was full of American soldiers as we were in the area occupied by the USA. I called his name but he never responded, so I gave up the idea. But the urge to exact revenge was always very strong, and it was an ever-present thought….

There was another incident, around the same time, where once again I was on a train near Munich. I was traveling with someone who belonged to the Bnei Akiva youth movement. He was a little older than me, and had a mischievous smile on his face. He told me he was "going to have a good time." Being relatively innocent at the time, I asked him what he meant. He told me he was going to have sex with a German prostitute for 50 marks, which at the time was just pennies. Germany was rife with poverty after the war and many German women engaged in prostitution for pennies. We relished the idea of those Germans, some of whom were probably the daughters of Nazis who had murdered Jews during the war, were now selling their bodies to the Jewish "subhumans". In effect, therefore, "screwing" the Germans as we so eloquently called it, was also a form of retribution.

I also took revenge on certain Ukrainian collaborators after the war, when I turned them over to the NKVD. I have no qualms about it whatsoever. I did whatever I could to take revenge and I would have done more if I could have… the only thing I feel guilty about is not dying along with my family, especially my sister.

Looking back, however, I didn't derive much satisfaction from taking revenge. It may have felt good in the moment – you tell yourself you punished a murderer and feel a tinge of satisfaction – but at the end of the day it doesn't give you much. Sending someone to Siberia or having them executed for their atrocious crimes is just revenge indeed, but it doesn't bring back my loved ones and does nothing to dull the pain.

Unfortunately, I was too young to be a soldier or a partisan, so I didn't get to kill Germans or Ukrainians myself, but I did what I could and can only regret not doing more.

But I would say that the greatest revenge of all is staying alive and building a family.

**The next dilemma is titled "Like lambs to the slaughter". After the war it was common to hear Israelis refer to the Jews who died in the Holocaust by saying they "went like lambs to the slaughter". Is it morally justified to say something like that about the victims?**

What does that phrase even mean? Can you really comprehend it? I can't. It would mean that the Jews had reached such a state of despair that they were unwilling to go on living, so they didn't even think to resist…

**The next dilemma is titled the "Reparations Dilemma". In 1953 an agreement was signed between Israel and West Germany under which the latter agreed to pay reparations**

to the State of Israel and to the Holocaust victims personally. Do you recall the debate in Israel over the subject of German reparations?

Yes, I lived in Mashabei Sadeh at the time. The reparations were collectively pooled and the money went to the kibbutz. When Kibbutz Shamir was privatized in 2002, I started receiving the money personally.

**What are your thoughts on the debate itself?**

You know, I always say – best get whatever we can from the Germans.

**Do you still receive reparations from Germany?**

I receive a form of pension payment totaling 240 euros per month. Every Holocaust survivor recognized as such by the Germans receives the same payment for life. There was a German fellow who used to live on Shamir named Ludwig – I believe you knew him – who was good friends with Gadi Lahav, my son-in-law. He went with me to the bank and filled out the forms in German so I could receive the payment. I have a lot of letters I've received from the Germans, each year they want to know if I'm still alive (laughs). They send me a letter and I have to send one back so they know they still have to pay. I also get a stipend from the Israeli Finance Ministry.

**What do you receive a stipend for?**

For being a Holocaust survivor and due to the fact that I have 65% disability.

**Why do you get disability allowance?**

In the forest during the war I was healthy, but a short while after liberation I contracted tuberculosis. Many survivors suffered from it due to the harsh conditions during the war. Generally, you should know that all survivors have certain degrees of mental and physical health problems. All of them! In the mid-1950s, I was hospitalized because of tuberculosis. I was admitted to "Meir" Hospital in Kfar Sava, where they had a department specializing in pulmonary diseases. I was there for about a year, and eventually had a lobectomy in "Tel Hashomer" Hospital. I also have a hearing deficiency in my left ear, and am medically classified as partially deaf. I also have diabetes now, which caused the social security to increase my disability allowance. They didn't really want to, on account of so much time having passed since the war, but I managed to convince them that it was due to the war and they approved it (winks).

**What do you think of Israel-Germany relations? Should they have ever been normalized?**

The Germans have always historically wished to rule the east. During the war it was to annex Poland and Russia. It was true in medieval times, it was true in the first World War, and it was true in the second. And the Germans' lust to conquer the east has not waned. The current German chancellor Angela Merkel uses no weapons to satisfy this need. The Germans de facto control Europe – many less economically robust countries turn to them for financial aid, and that's the way the Germans control the continent – no army required. It's as if they're saying, "Even after we killed all the Jews, we still rule Europe." Our former prime minister Netanyahu approached the Germans, and Merkel treated him like a feather in her cap. She's an older woman who never got married or had children. She's not too bad, mind you. Netanyahu came to her with all his ministers and she gets to brag about how she helps Israel, and it legitimizes her regime. It's like Germany is the car and Israel is the keyring. I may be philosophizing here, but it's true... Merkel is an impressive woman, she rules quietly. All the ministers are eager for her to speak to them, and just look at the way she runs the country. Historically speaking, you can see how the Nazis killing all the Jews benefited their grandchildren and great-grandchildren. The older Germans who took part in the Holocaust, the flesh and blood of the Wehrmacht and the SS, are mostly long gone – they would have to be over 90 years old by now. But those few who are still alive have got to be happy with the situation. What Kaiser Wilhelm II couldn't achieve in World War I, and what Hitler could not achieve in World War II, is happening now. Think about it! Today Germans travel all over Europe, the whole continent is wide open to them... they may not be particularly liked, but you can be certain that their money is needed. Having good relations with the Germans and having their financial support is a good thing.

During the Holocaust, they used to sing their national anthem – Deutschland *über alles* (Germany above all) – and to this day they still sing it and have those aspirations of a greater Germany.

**Outwardly, many Germans say they love Israel and deeply regret the Holocaust, but what do you think their real thoughts are?**

I couldn't tell you for sure… antisemitism has by no means disappeared, but the Germans know what their ancestors did to the Jewish people and to the world, and they wish to atone for it. It's possible that deep down they think that Hitler killing all the Jews was a good thing, and it's a shame he didn't finish the job. They probably say those things after a few beers, when they're a little less cautious about what they say. In Hitler's January 1939 address, he warned that if war broke out in Europe because of the Jews, they would pay the price and be annihilated. He stated his intentions clearly in advance and prepared to execute them. Jewish leaders sensed the danger to a degree, they would pray for redemption and grew sick with worry, but they never actually did anything. If they had known what was about to happen, they surely would have acted differently. Even my own parents didn't think it would actually happen… they thought things would be hard, that food might be hard to come by – but having all the Jews murdered? The thought never crossed their minds. The sinister German scheming reached such extremes that the Jews couldn't possibly comprehend the extent of it. In that regard, the Jews were gullible as sheep. The butcher prepares to slaughter the lamb, but the lamb never knows… they never found a document with Hitler's signature decreeing that all Jews be killed, it was probably a verbal order. Hitler established the tools for the task: the SS, the Gestapo, the *Einsatzgruppen*. It was they who killed the Soviet and Eastern-European Jews in 1941-1942. Antisemitism has always been deeply rooted in German culture, despite the more uncouth and wild brand of antisemitism having its roots in eastern Europe. In Poland, the hatred of the Jews is as old as time. Hitler rode the wave of antisemitism and turned the mass killings into a scientific, administrative exercise. The widespread massacre of all the Jews was planned during the Wannsee Conference in Berlin in 1942. All the heads of the German security forces were there, eating and drinking with their blonde secretaries, plotting how they could most effectively get rid of the Jews. Up until then, the disorganized pogroms had only accounted for a relatively small number of victims; the Germans made it into a science. Hitler was the government, and Himmler, the head of the SS, was in charge of execution. It's hard to understand how it was the Germans of all people who implemented antisemitism in such a manner. Therefore, you can never really know what the Germans think and feel, and what they could possibly do to us if given another chance…

**What is your personal stance on Germany and the German people today?**

I hold no hatred toward them. I've visited Austria as well, even though Hitler was Austrian. I have nothing personally or racially against the Germans of today. These are not the same people that carried out the killings. At worst, they are their descendants. If my grandson were to marry a German woman I wouldn't look unfavorably upon the union, I'd even go to the wedding. My own son Yotam married a Ukrainian, so you never know. My grandson Noam has blond hair and blue eyes – perhaps he's the descendant of a Ukrainian who killed Jews 600 years ago? You can never know.

**The next dilemma is titled the "Kapo Dilemma". As you surely know, there were trials in the 1950s against Kapos who were charged with abuse and maltreatment of Jewish prisoners in the camps. What are your thoughts? Should those trials have been allowed to continue?**

I understand the desire for revenge and they found a few Jews who had been Kapos and made an example out of them. But what's the point? I remember one Kapo was sentenced to death but he received a stay of execution and eventually he didn't even go to prison. He defended himself by saying, "I was forced at gunpoint to do those things, what else could I have done?" The only man sentenced to death and executed in Israel was Adolf Eichmann, the Nazi officer who was the primary organizer of the massacre of the Jews. Humans are complicated beings. You could make a general argument that it is human evil that drives the evil actions that humans do. Evil and humanity go hand in hand. It was human evil that triggered the whole deal. The planners were German, and they executed their plans as well, but they had helpers from all over. People are naturally evil, they have a sinister side to them, but culture usually keeps those things at bay. The Germans extracted all of the suppressed human evil and used it as a weapon. Suddenly Germans, Poles and Ukrainians everywhere were allowed to run amok, uninhibited on their bloodthirsty quest to beat, humiliate, rape and kill – and that too in broad daylight, sanctioned by the government no less! That was the real tragedy – a massacre that was instigated by a government in broad daylight. The evil character of Haman from the book of Esther had plotted to kill all the Jews many years ago – so it wasn't a new idea. But it was the Nazi Germans who implemented the plans, and that's where the novelty of the Holocaust lies.

**The next dilemma is the "Israel Kasztner" dilemma. Kasztner was one of the leaders of the Jewish community in the Hungarian capital of Budapest, and for a while headed the Budapest Aid and Rescue Committee. He negotiated with Adolf Eichmann and other German officers for the release of Jews in exchange for trucks given by the allies to Germany. He also organized a train with 1,685 Jews on board to be sent to neutral Switzerland, with the approval of the Germans. After the war he was blamed by Hungarian Holocaust survivors for collaborating with the Germans and was tried for his crimes. Do you think he should have been blamed??**

Kasztner saved Jews, but to do so he had to work with the Germans. Malchiel Gruenwald, the Jew who accused him of collaborating with the Germans, only did it out of anger and resentment. He was looking for a scapegoat to blame for his family's death and found one. I don't think Kasztner did anything wrong. He made sure his own family was on that train and they all survived, but who would not have done so in his place? He also saved many other Jews besides his family. During the trial, the judge Benjamin Halevy said about him that he had "sold his soul to the devil", meaning the Nazis, and therefore declared him guilty in collaborating with the Nazis. Personally, I don't blame any Jew who worked with the Germans out of self-preservation. You can't judge a man based on forced collaboration. Someone who is attempting to save his own life, and by doing so saves many others, is not to blame in my view.

**The next dilemma is called the "Holocaust Comparison Dilemma". Do you think it is proper to compare the Holocaust to the genocides of other peoples?**

Absolutely. Genocide is genocide, no matter who the victims are, or where it happens. Even today, there is tribal warfare and genocide, the true extent of which is not even known. In 1994, a million people were massacred in Rwanda, but you know how it goes... "long absent, soon forgotten." David Ben Gurion, Israel's first prime minister, once said, "Arabs are killing Arabs – who are we to intervene?" African people kill other African people, Asian people kill other Asian people... you can't worry about everything. The Jews have always been a relatively humane nation, but people are naturally inclined to brutality. The human is a two-legged animal which still has a thirst for blood; the difference is we have been able to mostly keep it in check. Cain slew Abel, his own brother, out of envy. Greek mythology also depicts many murders. It is an innate urge, even if it is well hidden by the advent of culture. All men are potential murderers, but we have managed to police ourselves with government, the army, a police force, with courts of law, and culture. A person can't just murder whenever he likes. But morally speaking, if you were to murder someone you truly hated, you wouldn't really be sorry. Outwardly you might show remorse, but in a way you would be glad... once you start killing, there is an urge to do it again. It's been that way since the dawn of humanity. Stalin, leader of the Soviet

Union, mercilessly murdered millions of his own citizens. The "Holodomor", the Great Famine in 1932-1933, killed millions of Ukrainians due to the policies of Stalin's Communist regime. He deliberately confiscated a large proportion of their food to sell to the West and millions died because of him. The Ukrainians put the figure at around 20 million people, although it's hard to know exactly. The Ukrainians view that as genocide, and rightly so. The German Nazis made killing into an ideology. Ultimately, people care about themselves and their own family. Honestly, I don't care too much about the killings in Africa or Cambodia. I think it's a shame, but what's most important to me is that I'm not the one being killed. Anyone who tells you otherwise might seem like a noble person but it's just a facade. Would someone like that do anything other than talk? I doubt it…

**The final dilemma is called the "Resistance Type Dilemma". The full name of Holocaust Remembrance Day in Israel is "Holocaust and Heroism Remembrance Day". Do you think that the Jews who fought the Germans with arms should be remembered more than other forms of resistance?**

I've actually thought about this quite a bit. The "Holocaust" part is obvious, but "Heroism"? I'm not sure what that part is about. Was living in the ghetto a form of heroism? What about enduring torture or forced labor? Dying of starvation? What was the actual bravery? Was it those who took up arms? Were the partisans heroes? Should a person who died struggling for mere survival not be considered a hero? I'm not sure what the answer is, but it's definitely worth discussing!

---

**There's a school of thought which suggests that the partisans in the forests and members of the Jewish Underground who fought the Nazis in the ghettos, such as in the Warsaw Ghetto Uprising, were the true heroes. That is to say, if you took up arms against the Germans you were a hero, but if you were part of those who were massacred and shot at the killing pits, or if you escaped and hid, you were not a hero. What are your thoughts?**

Does bravery necessarily mean taking up arms and fighting? I never thought so… the Jews in the towns did not fight. Some escaped to the forests and the partisans were a phenomenon that only began much later, in 1942. There weren't that many of them, either. Most people were afraid for their lives, and preferred not to venture into danger. I don't think Antek and Zivia Zuckerman of Warsaw Ghetto fame were such great heroes. Antek looked like a Pole which helped him get by outside of the ghetto. Other than Warsaw, I am not aware of that many cases of Jews taking up arms in the ghettos. I know that in the Bereźne and Rivne ghettos, the Jews didn't fight, They were scared and acted out of self-preservation. There were some who joined the partisans, but I would call that mild heroism at best.

Most of the Jews from our area who survived were those who managed to escape to the USSR when the Germans rolled in, and others like me who hid out in the forests or were taken in by kind-hearted gentiles, but those were few and far between. Those few locals who were inclined to help the Jews were afraid to do so because the Nazis made it very clear that anyone caught harboring Jews would be killed as well.

Moreover, many of the Jews who escaped to the forests were later killed by the Ukrainians or the Germans.

To me, the true heroes are those Jews who kept their humanity. Those who lived to be saved and to save what could be saved. That is bravery to me. Hanging on, surviving, yet being able to not lose your humanity, to remain human even in the face of peril and death.

**What does "remaining human" mean to you?**

It means giving half of your 200 grams of bread to a Jew who is weaker than you, so that he may live. This is where a man truly scales the pinnacle of human morality. To me that is true heroism, that's my own philosophy. There weren't very many of those. Most didn't share their bread with anyone. A man needs to know that there is something to live for – he needs meaning and hope, which transcend the life force which is the engine of survival. Hope was what kept us warm during the cold nights in the forest. Without hope and meaning there would have been no survival. And without helping each other, we would not have survived. Helping your fellow Jew – that is what "remaining human" truly means.

**How did the Israelis treat you as a Holocaust survivor when you first arrived in Israel?**

There are some Holocaust survivors who say that when they first came here, they tried to tell people what they went through, but people didn't want to listen. That is true. People did not want to hear those horror stories, which is part of the reason I didn't speak much during my first years here. There was a wariness toward the survivors. It was as if they were asking how could we be alive, if the Nazis had killed everyone else? They thought, perhaps, that we had done something illicit or bought our way out of trouble, or done something immoral. Perhaps we had even collaborated with the Germans, turning over other Jews to the authorities in exchange for our freedom? In any case, Holocaust survivors were labeled "unkosher" because it wasn't clear how exactly they had escaped the Nazi death machine while all the others, including many strong people, had not. It was a sort of negative feedback loop: the survivors tried to tell their stories, people here didn't really want to hear them, so they stopped trying to talk about it, which increased suspicion toward them, as now they thought perhaps the survivors weren't talking because they had something to hide. The one point of difference was the children. We were viewed differently. People were mostly happy that there were children who had survived the horrors.

**What are the most powerful lessons to be learned from the Holocaust?**

Mainly the human lesson. On the one hand, humans are relatively weak, both physically and mentally – they submit quite easily to the dangers posed both by nature and by other men. On the other hand, humans possess the most incredible physical and mental powers which enable them to overcome the most trying difficulties.

Then there's the dichotomy of human good vs. human evil. The Ukrainians were motivated to apprehend Jews and hand them over to the Germans in exchange for salt. They were also negatively motivated to harbor Jews for fear of what the Germans would do if they were caught. Most of them hated the Jews anyway, so they did their fair share of killing Jews themselves. But on the other hand, without the good Ukrainians who fed the Jews occasionally, or provided shelter for a night here and there, or even for the long term – not even one Jew would have been saved.[7]

7. The descriptions of the dilemmas presented in this chapter are based on the literature review conducted as part of the doctoral research of Shay Efrat (Efrat, 2017)

# CHAPTER 10:
## THE SMILE ON MY SISTER'S FACE

**We are now entering the final phase of interviews, which is a sort of conclusion. In that spirit, I will now ask you a few questions.**

Go ahead.

**I have met Holocaust survivors who believe their personal story is not as important as the stories of others, and therefore refrain from telling it to their families, or from giving any sort of testimony at all. Did you yourself ever feel that way?**

Some survivors think their story is negligible because they weren't imprisoned in camps or ghettos, but sought refuge in the homes of kind-hearted gentiles and such. There were Polish Jews who escaped to Russia, but they suffered as well; the Russians sent many Jews to horrendous forced labor camps in Siberia. There were others who wandered Russia and died of starvation. I don't believe there are important stories and unimportant stories. Everything is important. My story, for example, is very important because in my town only 2.5% of the residents survived, and most of the survivors were those who managed to escape to Russia. Of those who were marched to the killing pits nobody survived, and of those who escaped to the forests, like myself, there were only a few dozen who made it out alive. There were a precious few who found shelter in the homes of good-hearted gentiles, and another handful who fought with the partisans, but that was it. Therefore, it is of great importance that anyone who survived should give testimony.

**Did you ever have difficulty giving interviews or testifying?**

No. It's always been important to me that I tell my story, and I've always accepted invitations and told it with no difficulty. That said, I do understand that not everyone is like that. Some people to this day still have great difficulty talking about it. Of course, anyone who is still alive today was a child back then, because anyone older is already gone... There are others who were infants and barely remember anything.

**You've mentioned memories quite often. Do you also have dreams about the Holocaust?**

Sure, I've dreamed about it a lot. The Holocaust goes with me wherever I go, I am a product of the Holocaust. I've had many bad dreams; about being afraid I would be killed, dreams of my family, difficult things like that. Often when I'm tired of life I ask myself, "Why did I survive?", because ultimately everyone has to die... There's a saying in Ukrainian which goes something like, "You lose the day you die", meaning the last day of your life is wasted. So there's this eternal burning question of, "Why was I the one who made it out alive?" Eventually, once you go, everything you've collected and learned during your life – it all goes with you. Nothing is left. What do I need that for? Why did I not go along with my mother and my sister? Perhaps it would have been better for me to go off and die rather than staying alive and contemplating death on a daily basis. Whenever I get into bed at night, there's a fear of death which creeps in. I tell myself, "No matter, you're old, they'll put you in the ground and nothing will be left." What did I need all this for? For memories? Suffering? Fighting? Sorrow? Pain? There are some people who have had real tragedies happen. They've lost children to illness or war. I can consider myself lucky, I have children and grandchildren who live nearby. But at the end of the day, there's nothing left once all is said and done. Life is no picnic, it's fraught with pain and suffering. Especially for those who endured the Holocaust, they have a heavy burden to carry. I carry it each day. Those who died, did so only once. I die every day again and again. I wash a cup in the sink, I remember my sister. I eat a slice of bread and think of my father. It's like that constantly. I usually don't mention these things, but they come back to haunt me incessantly.

**What is the most important thing in your life today?**

That's a difficult question, because there are so many things that are important to me. But I think the most important of all is family. Take it from someone who's already lost one family and knows its significance.

**Is there a message you'd like to pass on to us and to future generations?**

Look, life isn't eternal. We live on borrowed time, and we never know when our day will come. The question is: what do we do with our lives. When I was a small child, I didn't know what death was. I first became aware of it when I saw a funeral in the town. I remember crying and my mother patting me on the head, consoling me, saying, "Everyone dies, but don't worry, you still have plenty of time…" People have always believed there is an omnipotent God who controls everything, but as a Holocaust survivor I don't believe that. God is a fabrication dreamt up by humans so that they can have something to believe in. People have a need to be led and believe there's someone watching out for them, which is why they invented God, just as they had their idols during Pagan times. Humans are a flock in need of a shepherd, and that shepherd is God. The Jews in the Holocaust turned their eyes to the heavens, praying for salvation, but there was none forthcoming. Not because God was evil, because he didn't exist. Perhaps there's another explanation, that God does exist but he is powerless to control earthly events. In that case, what kind of God is he anyway? But I still think there's nothing up there. People have already been to space and seen there's nothing there but the usual natural things… no God. The Jews cried out for help and the Germans still killed them. They died with the sense that God had forsaken them, or perhaps punished them for their sins… perhaps they hadn't been good enough as Jews. That's wrong of course, they weren't guilty of anything. They're already dead, so this means nothing to them, but I know there's no God. For the Germans, Hitler was God, and the Nazi party and its race theory was their belief system. It was based on those beliefs that they carried out the orders of the party and the army, and just look at the terrible things they did! The Germans had allies such as Croatia and Romania, where the locals were the ones who carried out the killings. It was a way to finally get rid of all the Jews, and it stemmed from rabid antisemitism and Jew-hatred. Even in occupied countries such as Lithuania and Ukraine, as well as in Holland and France, there were locals who joined the SS and participated quite gladly in the massacre of the Jews. That's how much Jews are hated, and it has been that way throughout history. It's because the Jews are small and weak and scattered, and they annoy everyone else with their disproportionate success. Even the Allies who fought the Germans – the USSR, the USA, Britain and France – even they didn't lift a finger to save the Jews. So my message to my family and to Jews everywhere, is that we only have ourselves to trust. Remember the Holocaust and spread the message. This has always been my life's mission: Live to Tell the Tale!

**Is there something you haven't told me and wish to do so now?**

I've told you everything I could, but I would like to say a few words in conclusion. My story is in fact the story of my generation. It's the story of those who survived the Holocaust and rebuilt their lives, and it is incredibly important to tell it. After so much time has passed, your own faulty memory may alter some of the things that actually happened, because across the vast time lapse of dozens of years, it is difficult to convey what happened accurately. I am a product of the Holocaust, I survived it, it lives within me, but telling the stories accurately as I truly experienced them – that's something else entirely. Those who survived Auschwitz, for example, have their stories about what happened there, but I feel it's impossible to convey them accurately. You'd only be scratching the surface of what actually happened. I constantly try and comprehend the reality of my mother marching to her death alongside my six-year-old sister Buzha. A mother and her small child, standing in front of a German soldier or a Ukrainian collaborator who just shoots them dead. Perhaps they asked her, "Who should we shoot first? Your daughter or yourself?" It makes me feel sick and it stays with me constantly. I can give you another example: I walk on my treadmill and suddenly remember my uncle Pesach who survived the war and was later murdered by Ukrainian farmers. Those who died are dead, but those who survived carry the Holocaust constantly on their shoulders, like a snail carries its shell. I am the snail who carries the shell of the Holocaust on its back. Understanding what happened theoretically, is one thing. That's what you as a researcher can do. But actually experiencing it firsthand, that's a completely different thing, which only a survivor such as myself can understand. I see my mother constantly in my mind, but as time passes her face gets blurry, and I can no longer remember what she actually looked like. These things never actually leave me… I don't know what it's like for other survivors, but for me it's like a hump on my back.

**I believe all survivors feel that way, more or less.**

I believe that all survivors are haunted night and day by the powerful memories. Memories that are a constant reminder of where they came from. The problem facing Holocaust survivors is how to tell the stories so that people can understand them. Survivors wish to tell their story more than people listening want to hear them, because by doing so they feel more alive. I'm glad you're interviewing me and writing a book, because I'm always willing to talk about the Holocaust and it helps me to pass on the memories.

**It's a very important thing that you're doing.**

I've been doing it for years, and I would love my children and grandchildren to read my books as well. I'm very pleased that you're conducting thorough research on the Holocaust and writing about my story. My ideology is that the Holocaust should be written and talked about in order to memorialize those who died. Most of them died without leaving a testimony of some sort, so people should read and learn from those who can testify. I know that I need to keep working to tell my story, even if the memories aren't complete. I am certain that I survived in order to tell the story, and now you get to pass it on, which is incredibly important to me. I want to leave something after I'm gone, so that the Holocaust is always remembered.

**After all these years of memories and thoughts, what is the thing you remember most of all?**

You know, life is like a thread which slowly frays with time. The thing is that it can never be re-threaded. Memories grow distant with time. In a way I miss the forest, the smells, and the birch trees. I remember we used to sit around the fire on warmer nights telling jokes. We weren't afraid of the Germans because we were embedded deep in the forest. Besides, without a little camaraderie and humor we wouldn't have survived anyway, so we took a bit of a risk. The timeline is a bit hazy for me, but other than that, I remember pretty much everything.

My memories are like laundry on a clothesline. I wash them and hang them up again and again. Even though I'm an old man, I remember everything quite distinctly. I remember the day I walked back from the farmer's house to the Bereźne ghetto, and I brought a bag of green peas for my family. I will never forget the smile on my sister's face when she saw me… she was so happy! That smile will be etched in my soul for all eternity. After all these long years, my strongest memory is **the smile on my sister's face.**

**In closing, is there anything you would like to ask me?**

How were the interviews with the rest of my family?

**Very interesting and very moving! They all pitched in willingly and spoke openly, and were happy to contribute to the family story.**

Was it important to them?

**I'm certain it was. It was clear to me how much you mean to them, and their need to get to know your story better in order to pass it on was also apparent. After all, they went with you to Bereźne and agreed to be interviewed for a book which is mostly about you, entailing quite a bit of exposure for them… it means a lot!**

I'm glad to hear it. We never really discussed how each of them feels. I have many questions: Is my story important to them? Do they live with it in a way? Have they been affected by my stories? Do they see themselves as a part of me, the primeval relic from the Holocaust? Do they feel an obligation towards me to remember what happened? Do they appreciate me for having endured the Holocaust, for having survived all those ordeals? What do they think of their father, their grandfather who lived through bitterly cold winters in the forests, and went through hell, but yet leads a normal family life with them these days? We never discuss any of that.

**I hope you still get a chance to talk those things through. I feel they have a lot of appreciation and a sense of obligation toward you, both in an emotional sense and from a family standpoint. You are incredibly important to the family. Generally speaking, I think they feel obligated to memorialize the events of the Holocaust. Each has their own story, and the sum of all the parts is a fascinating, moving multi-generational family story.**

In my mind it's like a tree which branches out every which way. I am the old tree which branches out, and those branches in turn also branch out. They absorbed the Holocaust from a young age because I told them the stories very early on. Both my children and my grandchildren were made aware of these stories at an early age. So from that perspective I've managed to fulfill my calling, which is to tell the story of the Holocaust and pass on the memories. In that sense I have been blessed to live and tell the tale, and to have written my books and poems to memorialize the dead is a great success for me. I can be content with that, but at my very core I am not happy and not satisfied. I haven't managed to fill the voids left in me; I still feel a sense of hunger to complete something which may never be completed. I can't rest on my laurels; I can't truly enjoy my personal successes. I never really experience true unbridled joy, and I guess that's just not a possibility for someone who lost his entire family in the Holocaust.

**I want to thank you for these interviews, and to express my gratitude that I got to know you. May you live long and experience only joy and satisfaction from your children, your grandchildren and your great-grandchildren.**

Thank you, Shay, for investing so much time and effort in my story and my family's story!

# PART II – A FAMILY'S STORY

This part includes the personal stories of Shmuel's family members who tell about him and themselves in the shadow of the Holocaust.

## CHAPTER 11:
## THE STORY OF NATAN SUCHA

**"I always sensed the concern"**

Natan is Shmuel and Bracha's second child, younger sister to Livya and older brother to Yotam. He is married to Miri. The couple have three daughters: Nitzan, Rotem and Eden.

I'd like to start my story with our trip with Dad to Bereźne in 2002. I'm not quite sure who came up with the idea. I think there were suggestions of "follow your roots" trips, and several Holocaust survivors' groups got together and organized the trips. Dad didn't really ask me if I wanted to come along. He heard about the group tour being organized, and simply said: "You're going to come with me and learn about your roots". It was not a request.

It was a seven-day organized trip that we didn't plan, but rather tagged along. The first trip to Bereźne included myself with Dad, Mom, and Yotam, my younger brother. When we got to his hometown of Bereźne, he searched for his old house but couldn't find it. In fact, he couldn't really remember where it had been. He also was unsuccessful in his attempt to locate any certificates, photographs, or personal items which he had hoped somehow to find. However, there was another village we visited, where he managed to find a woman who was the daughter of the farmer he had stayed with before the massacre of the Jews. She said she remembered him and kissed him. The truth is that it was during this trip that I became closer to my father and to the history of the family. Thanks to this trip, the story of the Holocaust meant more to me, and I felt personally touched by it. The trip was a powerful experience.

The places we visited had plenty of memorials and cemeteries. His mother's family was from the village of Mezhyrich. While we were there, he searched for tombstones with the name "Fishman", because that was her maiden name. We found several, but he wasn't sure if they were from our family or not, because he didn't know their first names. Throughout the trip he spoke very eloquently and explained what had happened in each place. We saw the area where he hid out in the forest, and he told us how he found shelter among the trees and bathed in the ashes from the fire. He tells those stories much better than I do.

I remember being very touched after hearing the stories and seeing the places he had been in. It's been many years since then, but when I watch the videos I shot during the trip, it takes me back. He talked constantly throughout the journey, and I was there to capture everything. On the bus he would take the microphone and talk for hours... he barely let the guide get a word in! He knows his history, and he told us about how the Germans made sure the Jews suffered every step of the way, even in death. He told us that the Ukrainian Jews were often killed by local Ukrainian Nazi collaborators. At first, when the Germans arrived, they concentrated their efforts on fighting the Russians; they left the Jews alone. He told me that once he fixed a bicycle for a German soldier and got his finger caught in the chain. When the German soldier saw his gushing wound, he rushed to his aid and bandaged the wound. But soon the attitude changed and the Germans started setting up ghettos and killing people. The Bereźne ghetto wasn't completely sealed; people could have escaped if they wanted to, and would have – had they foreseen what was going to happen. Dad told us that his father could easily have moved the family to Russia, but they never believed that they would actually need to do so.

One of the more fortuitous encounters on this trip was with Dasha, the future wife of my younger brother Yotam. At the time she was staying in Rivne with her aunt; we had joined another family of Bereźne survivors who were on the trip on a visit to her aunt's house, and Dasha was there. We also visited the Babi Yar massacre site in Kyiv, and the Jewish Center in Uman. My parents made three trips to Ukraine, and I remember that they were moved the most by the first one (the trip I was on in 2002) – they were younger at the time. I bonded with them and with my brother Yotam, and it was really a great trip!

As a boy I remember hearing many stories from my father: The story of how he saw his mother and sister for the final time, when his mother berated him for coming back to the ghetto and sent him back to the farmer's house he had been staying at; the story of how his uncle was murdered while going to retrieve some clothes after the war; and many others. But what I remember most about my childhood is his constant worry that I would be hurt somehow. It's a fear that I can't shake to this day. It has really stuck with me – an uncontrollable anxiety and fear that he passed on to me, probably more so than my sister Livya or my brother Yotam. I've always been worried of getting sick, or falling, or injuring myself, or dying. I believe it's because of my father's concerns for me as a child. I did my military service in the Paratroopers' Brigade, and I felt it there just as strongly. Even today there are some situations in which I'm overwhelmed with anxiety. Sometimes I overcorrect in the other direction, almost going out of my way to endanger myself. For example, when mountain bike riding, I tend to be overconfident and get into risky situations. Sometimes I don't understand why I worry so much. I guess it's because he passed it on to me somehow. Even though in my daily life I'm not as anxious anymore, there's still a subconscious component to it. It's not as if he was always telling me that something would happen, but I always sensed the concern. As a boy, I also watched him worry over my younger brother Yotam. His concern manifests particularly around issues such as food – he always saves whatever leftovers he can, and never leaves anything on his plate. He also has an issue with money. He says he doesn't like to spend it, but it would be more accurate to say that he just saves whatever money he can, simply due to the fear of not having enough. He saves whatever he has and hoards everything, even small change. He scrimps and saves, and spends as little as possible – just like the old generation. In the collectivist kibbutzim of the past, people didn't have much money; whatever they got, they saved. When he worked as a journalist he used to get a small per diem stipend, but he preferred to take a sandwich from the dining room so he could save the money.

I guess there's nothing one can do about such things, they're so deeply ingrained that they get passed on to the next generation. Even now, at a time where I have all I need and more than enough money, I still find myself forgoing a purchase so I can save the money.

My mother, on the other hand, was nothing like him. She was astute with money, but she also would spend it eventually. Any material possession I wanted as a child, I had to fight for with my parents – and it was always my mother who eventually yielded.

Nowadays, they're more liberal with giving money to their children and grandchildren, as they're much older and have social security, pensions, and reparations as Holocaust survivors.

I think that the Holocaust is still the issue that affects my father more than anything else. He can't help it. If he's alone in the house he won't turn on the air conditioner, because it costs money to run. If I tell him to turn it on, he'll say he's not hot. He'd rather sit in his underwear than turn it on. And in the winter he sits in doors with a sweater, so he doesn't get cold. I assume he really doesn't get cold, having lived through those freezing winters in the forests.

These are things that get passed on from generation to generation. Even if I had told myself that I wouldn't become like him, it's never completely unavoidable. I have money but I save it and act as if I have none. I know it's irrational but that's just the way it is.

There are also positive traits that I inherited from him, such as a burning desire to succeed in life. He served as a great example to me on that front, because he always managed to achieve what he desired. He wanted to become a journalist, and he succeeded – despite the language difficulties. He worked as a journalist for Al *Hamishmar*. He wanted to become a writer, and he did that too!

He's very expressive and eloquent, both verbally and in writing. He never really went to school after about the fourth or fifth grade, when the war started. He came to Israel at the age of seventeen. His general knowledge is impressive, especially in history. He can't remember what he did yesterday, but he'll accurately recite stories from the war!

I remember the years he worked in the apple orchard on the kibbutz. His apple picking groups always had the highest volume of all the groups. He loves trees and fruit picking season, he always has. Not long ago I took him tomato picking. He was so enthusiastic! By the time I had ten tomatoes in my basket, he already had one hundred!

When I was a child, my father told me some stories about the Holocaust, but it wasn't much. In recent years he's opened up more, especially about how much he thinks of his sister and mother. Ever since my mother got sick, I've become closer to them and we visit them more often. I spend more time with Dad now, and he's started to talk more. I've come to understand how difficult the topic of the Holocaust is for him. His stories are captivating. He always says he can picture his little sister and his mother. Once he starts talking, I can listen to him for hours, and it brings us closer together. I guess he's making up for our childhood, when he never really spoke much about it. I never ask him to start talking about it; it always has to come from him first. But once he gets going, it's never dull, and never gets boring. I also can't seem to remember it all. Each time I hear the stories, it's as if I'm hearing them for the first time. My daughters have also heard some stories about the Holocaust, although to a lesser extent. I'm not sure how much they actually remember, but it was important to him that the grandchildren accompany him on the family roots trips to Bereźne. My daughter Nitzan did join him on one of the trips. On Holocaust Memorial Day, he used to come and tell his story at the elementary school and the regional high school where my daughters went.

He told us that after the massacre of the Jews, the farmer who had taken him in forced him to leave because he was afraid that the Germans would kill him if they found out he was harboring Jews. He fled to the forest, an eleven or twelve-year-old boy, all alone, until he found several groups of Jews to live with. He always tells the story of his uncle Pesach, whom he met after liberation. Pesach told him, "Now I will be a father to you," and embraced him. Imagine the excitement for a young boy, finding his one surviving relative! And then he was murdered when he went to get his belongings from one of the farmers. That's the story he recounts most of all, especially the part about where he went back with Russian soldiers and pointed the murderer out to them.

He also tells a story of being hunted by the Germans in the forest. The soldiers used hounds to sniff them out, and my father ran and tripped in the snow, playing dead when one of the dogs caught him. The soldier who approached him was probably not German, and despite seeing he was alive decided not to kill him. He would always say, "If they didn't kill me at that point, I must be invincible." And yet he's also extremely anxious, and I'm that way too. I ride my bicycle on my own and take risks without any fear at all, but on the other hand, I find I'm extremely anxious about other matters.

When you think of it, my father grew up without parents from a very young age. He only has about seven years' worth of memories from his family. I grew up in a communal children's home on the kibbutz. I find it to be an inappropriate way of raising children, where parents rarely see their children. My mother was also orphaned at the age of ten, and by the age of fifteen, she had already immigrated to Israel. She doesn't even know exactly how her own mother died. But my mother hadn't suffered the way my father had, and our relationship with her was more open. If I needed to talk with one of them, it was usually easier to speak with my mother, because my father was more withdrawn and introspective.

These days, I visit my parents much more often than in the past, and I help with whatever they need. I will drop everything and come at any hour if they need help. When I see my brother Yotam, he always tells me what a good son I am to them. It does feel good to know that I've been spending more time with them and helping them more. My wife Miri says, "You've finally gained your parents, and they've gained you." But as far as I'm concerned, it's obvious that I should be doing this. Because if I don't, who will? And I already help others, so shouldn't I help them more than anyone?

My mother has been unwell over the past few years and my father takes care of her. As old and as tired as he is, I can still see the warrior qualities in him. He walks on the treadmill for an hour each day. Sometimes he forgets he exercised in the morning, so he does it again in the afternoon. My mother reminds him of everything, and despite their difficulties with her illness, they still live in harmony.

# CHAPTER 12:
# THE STORY OF LIVYA LAHAV

**"My dad is shadowed by anxiety"**

Livya Lahav is the eldest daughter of Bracha and Shmuel Sucha. She is married to Gadi. Their children are Guy, Adi, and May. They are also grandparents to Yahli-Yehudit and Ziv, Guy's children.

**Part One – My dad:**

I'd have to dig deep in my memory to be able to tell you about what it was like growing up as a Holocaust survivor's daughter. There were stories that my father told about relatives that had been murdered. I don't remember how old I was when it started, but I remember the stories were always disjointed. A few years ago, my husband Gadi and I sat together and tried to document the family history – the names on the family tree and the order of the events in Dad's stories – but we couldn't do it. The memories and descriptions were too jumbled, probably because these are mostly childhood memories.

For example, he told us that his father took him to a farmer from another village who he used to trade with so he would hide him. At a certain point the farmer said he couldn't harbor him anymore because it was too dangerous, and so he started to wander the forest alone, looking for food and thinking he was the last Jewish child alive in the world. He would eat mushrooms and wild berries, and dug a little trench to hide in. At night he would cover himself with leaves in lieu of a blanket.

Another story I've heard more than once is about the time he snuck into a farmer's house, stole some vegetables and ran away. There was also another time where a farmer gave him some food and let him stay the night. In the morning, he overheard the farmer and his wife discussing about turning him over to the Nazis in exchange for a bag of salt, and he managed to escape at the last minute. Many times he told us of the last time he saw his family. He always described it with such strong emotions of sorrow and yearning. He walked all the way from the village he was staying at to go and visit his family in the ghetto. He brought them a bag of peas, and when his sister saw him she was so happy. He wanted to stay with them, but his mother forbade him to stay and sent him back to the farmer in the village. His father wasn't home at the time, and he never saw him again. It was the final image he had of his family. He later heard from the farmer that all the Jews in the town had been murdered.

Most of the stories he told us were about the Holocaust, but there were also a few stories of childhood experiences, like the foods his father liked to eat, and how much he liked to drink vodka in the winter. There were many disjointed and jumbled stories and associative images, and we always asked questions for clarification.

My father's memories are the confused memories of a small child. It's important to understand that the experiences which affect one's emotions are embedded differently in one's memory. It makes a difference whether the testimonies are those of a child or those of an adult, and my father was a child during the Holocaust. Even now, there's a side of him that is somewhat childish, although he does remember quite a few details.

It is often difficult to find the common thread in his stories, but the specific events he recounts are very accurate and clear. He's also very well-versed in history, and he fits his own stories within that history. He is very knowledgeable.

When we were children, he used to tell us multi-part stories he had invented – they weren't related to the Holocaust – and we always waited excitedly for the next part. I can't remember any of those stories now, I only remember we sat there riveted. It's a shame he never recorded them. He's always been an excellent storyteller. There's something about the way he speaks which fascinates the listener. The problem is that because his thought process is so associative, he loses the common thread of the stories on the Holocaust.

The fact that he's a survivor who endured all those experiences had a huge impact on the way he raised us and treated us as children. As a child, I always sensed the anxiety around him. Dad is shadowed by anxiety, and throughout our childhood there was a sense of foreboding, like something horrible might happen to us. I remember he used to pick up the newspaper and read me various reports on rapes so that I would be afraid to hitchhike or talk to strangers. When there was a fight and one of my brothers ran out of the house for a moment, he was certain he had fallen into a pothole and died, and would exclaim, "Our child is dead!" It happened multiple times, and I would always try and calm him down and tell him that nothing was wrong. He would respond, "But how do you know?"

My father lived with a perpetual sense of anxiety. He used to say that after being surprised with the worst possible news as a child, he never wanted to be surprised again. He explained that he would constantly imagine the worst possible things that could happen to the family. Our parents – especially our father – always gave us a sense that death was right around the corner. The intense anxiety is indescribable. He still feels dread and anxiety to this day, albeit not at the same level. He's become somewhat calmer. Today he's more anxious about my mother because she's ill. He's not as anxious about myself or my brother Natan, although he does have more concerns about my youngest brother Yotam, his wife Dasha, and their children. Perhaps this is due to the fact that – unlike Natan and myself – they don't live in Shamir, and he doesn't see them as often.

But when we were children the anxiety was horrible; he constantly thought his children were going to die. I had to work very hard to shed the anxiety myself. It wasn't easy at all, and it took many years, a lot of work, and help from my husband Gadi.

The stories and characters of his past are reappearing now, more so than in the past. When he was younger, he was busier and had less time for thinking, but even today he's still very much connected with current events. He's deaf in one ear, so he puts the radio to his one good ear and listens to the news. The older he gets, the more he thinks of the family he lost in the Holocaust. He talks about how the memories constantly haunt him. You can see it in the poems he wrote about his parents and his sister. And yet he doesn't like to talk about anything that troubles him in the here and now. If our mother tells us he isn't feeling well, he berates her for telling us.

I was shocked when I first learned how big the family was and how they were all just wiped out. We would have been a very large family today if they had survived. His mother's side of the family was small, but on his father's side there were six brothers, all married with children. My father told me that his maternal grandfather emigrated to Canada in the 1930s and was never found. He constantly talks about the family he has in Canada and how he would love to find them. Every time he talks about the past, there's a new story I've never heard before. Hopefully this book will help us make some sense of all the stories. Perhaps if I had sat and written down all the stories he told us over the years, there'd be more of them. The problem was that we never got any clear answers to any of our questions, because of how associative he is.

My husband Gadi feels the same away about his parents, who are also Holocaust survivors. Most survivors have an emotional need to suppress the past. There were also so many things to deal with once they got to Israel, and they wished to start a new life with a clean slate. All of these things together impact the desire and the ability to recount stories of the past. When our son Guy had to write a family roots project for his Bar Mitzvah, Gadi took the opportunity to interview his parents so he could learn more. I think it's probably the first time he compiled their memories in an organized manner.

Alongside their need to suppress the past, many survivors felt the need to release the pent-up emotions through stories or art in various forms. However, it's important to remember that their lives here were very demanding. My parents lived on the kibbutz which had a set of collectivist values which place more importance on the here and now than on the past, and aspired to erase the dark shadows of the Holocaust. This stemmed from the necessity for development of the infant state of Israel, and also a cultural reluctance to discuss the Holocaust. I mentioned the family roots project my son Guy did for his Bar Mitzvah; my mother's story is the shortest part of it – a concise, laconic description. Gadi wanted his father to recount his stories but he never managed to get him to talk about it. His father just couldn't do it... he had barely survived the ordeal. By the end of the war he was a "Muselmann"[8] (human skeleton) with an endless list of diseases. He was hospitalized and then stayed at a sanatorium in Switzerland for three years before he recovered. He died at a relatively young age from cirrhosis of the liver due to hepatitis. In truth it was really due to the war[9].

Even though Gadi doesn't say much about his parents' anxiety when he was a child, I do know his mother has an issue with food. It's similar to my father's fear that there won't be enough food. On the other hand, Gadi's parents weren't as uptight about their children when they were growing up. It could be that my father's experience in the forest caused him to be more anxious, or perhaps it's something genetic. Either way it seemed that, surprisingly enough, Gadi's parents weren't as uptight. I've known them long enough to be sure. It's quite unbelievable to think how much the fear of death has hovered over my father's

---

8. "Muselmann" - a term used amongst Jewish prisoners of the concentration camps due to their extreme emaciation.

9. Many Holocaust survivors died at relatively young ages due to diseases and injuries they had received during the Holocaust. Even those who lived longer suffered from various levels of physical and emotional afflictions.

head the whole time. And then there's the whole other side of him, where he says that if he didn't die in the Holocaust, he must be invincible… a kind of robust faith that protects him. How did he manage to survive it all? It really is a fascinating question.

When Dad escaped to the forest, he was about eleven or twelve years old, he isn't quite sure himself. I think that because my father was so young, the whole experience shaped who he became thereafter, including the everlasting dread of death. Gadi's parents – who were from Hungary – were somewhat older. The Nazis also came to Hungary in 1944, much later than they came to Poland. Gadi's father was out looking for work when he was caught. He always said that he could have hidden if the information about the Nazis had been shared. He was always angry at Israel Kasztner of the Budapest Aid and Rescue Committee, claiming he didn't share the information about the impending massacre with the rest of the Jews. His mother and younger brother managed to hide and weren't caught. Gadi's mother was fifteen years old when the Nazis took her with her family to Auschwitz. Her family was from Czechoslovakia, where the Holocaust began relatively early. The Jews of Slovakia were among the first to be sent to Auschwitz in 1942, but her parents fled to the Hungarian border and were apprehended in 1944. They were a wealthy upper class family, which helped them to survive.

I don't think my father is as anxious about his grandchildren as he was about us as children. He's also warmer towards them. He hugs them often, which is something he had more difficulty doing with us. However, he still doesn't manage to keep in constant touch with them. He's always happy to see them when they visit him, but that's where it ends. The relationship is up to the grandchildren. He doesn't reach out, and I think that it has to do with his difficulty to develop profound relationships with people. It's part of the mental and emotional ramifications of the Holocaust.

Dad feels that he has a responsibility to tell the story of the Holocaust. He feels that because he is the only one left from his family, he has a duty to "pass on the torch", so to speak. He carries the dead around with him wherever he goes and doesn't stay in touch as much with his living relatives, nor does he notice how his attitude affects them in that regard.

I've read his poems about the Holocaust many times. We used to read them together and discuss them. At first he'd let me read them and make some corrections, and at some point he turned to others. I found it too hard to be constantly exposed to the subject matter. The poems are basically a series of images describing feelings and emotions, intertwined with memories. After all, poems aren't always the easiest thing to understand…

Throughout the years, I never really told my children in great detail about what it was like to grow up as children of Holocaust survivors. I had no desire to pass on the negative experience to my children, but I did tell them some things when it was relevant.

**Part Two – The Trip to Bereźne:**
Over the years, my father organized three trips to his hometown of Bereźne in search of his family roots. On the first trip, in 2002, he and my mother were joined by my younger brothers Natan and Yotam. On the second trip, in 2005, I joined them along with my son Guy. And on the third trip, in 2008, they were joined by my daughter Adi and Natan's daughter Nitzan. When we went in 2005, there was an unveiling ceremony for the Jewish memorial in Bereźne, paid for by the survivors living in Israel. Dad spoke at the ceremony about his murdered family members and mentioned their names. That's when the realization hit me – they had such a big family! His father had six siblings, all married with children – and yet my father was the only one left standing when it was all said and done. He was only a boy when it happened, but he remembers so many names. As a Jewish survivor, he feels a duty to remember and to memorialize. His urge to put everything in writing also stems from the desire to memorialize his family.

Their first trip to Bereźne was during the school year, and I couldn't go along because I worked as a kindergarten teacher. I joined the second trip with my son Guy, because it was during the summer holidays and he was just about to be drafted into the army. The trip was organized by a fellow survivor named Yonah Keller. It was very important to Dad that Guy join us, because he felt that the grandchildren should go there as well. It was a very emotional and difficult trip, but it was very meaningful. During the trip, we heard stories from all the people in the group. We saw the towns, the landscapes, the schools, and the mass graves. There were many witnesses and they all gave testimony. I videotaped people telling the stories of what happened to them and their families. There were other second- and third-generation survivors there as well.

The most difficult place to visit was in Rivne, the biggest city in the area. There's a huge memorial there built in the shape of a circle, and comprised of tombstones for all the families that were murdered. Hundreds and hundreds of little tombstones as far as the eye can see… and as you walk from tombstone to tombstone, you can actually sense the sheer number of people that were murdered, it was awful!

Not all the people in the tour group were from Bereźne. There were others from a nearby village, which also had a mass grave. Some of the stories told by the local gentiles were truly horrifying. They told us that for three days there was the sound of gunfire from the forest, until they had finished killing everyone. The farmers said their cows refused to go near the area because of the smell of blood.

When you walk in those areas you are literally walking on a gravesite. The Germans – helped by the Ukrainians – murdered everyone. I decided I would never go back there, but my father did want to go back. He said that it was still his homeland. Throughout the trip he kept searching for remnants of his past: his birth certificate, his house, the people he knew… He was so moved by the whole experience that his voice grew hoarse and he couldn't speak.

He also searched for the house of Soltus, the farmer who had let him stay with him for a while in Kurhany. We arrived there and found an old lady – I'm not sure how much she actually remembered – but my father was so excited to meet her. He couldn't find any relics in Bereźne because the town hall building had burned down along with all the documents.

**Part Three – My Mother:**

My mother never spoke much about her childhood. Where she grew up in southern Romania, the Jews weren't massacred by the Germans. The local antisemitic Romanians treated the Jews very poorly, but there were no mass killings. I remember she told me once that she was thrown off a bus and was injured. She either doesn't remember much, or chooses not to tell as much. I know that her own father was subjected to forced labor as a roofer during the war. Her parents both died of disease and starvation during the Holocaust. They had lived in Ploieşti, not far from the capital Bucharest. My mother and her siblings had a very difficult childhood. When her father died of tuberculosis at the age of thirty-five, her mother remained a single mother of four. She worked hard as a seamstress, but it wasn't enough and so the children had to drop out of school and go to work. My mother had been an outstanding student and was tasked with teaching other younger children in the afternoons. The local Jewish community wanted to pay for her to stay and teach alongside her own studies, but the family moved to Galați where her mother's sisters lived. And so at age eleven, my mother started working as a seamstress and her ten-year-old brother worked for a local miller selling matches on the streets. Later on, my grandmother also died of tuberculosis, and my mother's younger brother and sister were taken to an orphanage. My mother was now in charge of the household, where she continued to work and take care of her brother who also stayed with her. She was only fourteen years old when the war ended, and her aunts encouraged her to immigrate to Palestine. Postwar Romania was a bleak place to live – rife with starvation, poverty, and disease. My mother started going to HaShomer Hatzair youth movement meetings, became a Zionist, and eventually left Romania in 1947 and immigrated to Palestine. At fifteen years of age, after three months at the detention camp in Cyprus, she finally made it here. She always said that the reason she came to Israel was that her mother's sisters told her that she would be able to help her siblings if she came here. Meanwhile, her brother who stayed in Romania contracted tuberculosis, and she sent him medication from Israel. Although she never spoke of it, I think she harbors suppressed feelings of guilt due to the fact that she, as the eldest sister, abandoned her family and made Aliyah (immigrated to Israel).

She doesn't remember much anymore, either due to age or due to the fact that she just doesn't want to remember. She does, however, remember the day-to-day things that my father tends to forget. He remembers the past and she remembers the present. We once had a reunion with my mother's family, and her brother filled in the blanks of her family's story back in Romania. My mother spoke very little, but it was enough to let us know how difficult it had been for her.

As a child, I remember wanting to hear more from her, and I would occasionally ask, but she rarely ever spoke about herself. Perhaps she was trying to protect us, or she wanted to concentrate on being in a new, more positive place. Perhaps she never came to terms with her decision to come to Israel and leave her siblings behind.

# CHAPTER 13:
# THE STORY OF GADI LAHAV

**"I did not grow up a 'second-generation survivor'"**

I was born and raised in Ramat Gan. My wife Livya and I made our home in Shamir, and had three wonderful children: Guy, Adi, and May. Guy is married to Aviva and they have a daughter named Yahli as well as a son named Ziv.

**Part 1 – Shmuel**

The first time I met Shmuel in his home, was in the summer of 1977. He spoke with a unique sense of humor laced with metaphors and expressions from different fields of interest, and it was certainly entertaining. He spoke about a water polo game between our kibbutz's team and a local rival. He didn't even look at me while he was talking, but merely threw things out in a funny manner. I was there with his daughter Livya, who was my girlfriend at the time. He knew who I was, and perhaps there was a moment of slight awkwardness – perhaps he didn't quite know how to approach me. I remember him sitting around and cracking jokes. I assume that this was his way of getting to know someone, as if to say, "This is me, I'm a funny, humorous guy." His sentences were formulated in a way I had never heard before. For example, he was talking about someone who lived on the kibbutz, and described him as "someone who packs his entire system of values into a small suitcase and carries it around." That's something you don't usually hear, and I found myself wondering what he meant: did the man have almost no values at all, or did he stick to them all the time?

My personal connection to the Holocaust was often manifested through meetings and gatherings in the Sucha home, which often included Shmuel discussing his Holocaust experiences. He has a knack for being fresh and surprising, combining imagery in a unique way and peppering everything with humor. Each time he told us something new we hadn't heard before. And each time he told the story, it was told in a new way. Like a skilled baker, he "kneads" the language and contorts it into almost impossible combinations of names, concepts, situations, times, and places. He remembers many things from the past, and in great detail too. The experience of the Holocaust is indelibly imprinted on him. He's a poet who possesses a rich world of imagery, and if he wanted to, he could write about anything. Shmulik was a journalist, and over the years he cultivated a uniquely interesting viewpoint on all things political, social or cultural. Poetry is his safe space, his comfort zone – and as far as imagery is concerned, he always circles back to the forest and the trees, and the sensations they evoke within him. There's something very depressing about his poems; it's hard to believe that the person who wrote them possesses such an extraordinary sense of humor.

There's a significant contrast between the way he tells stories of the Holocaust and the way he writes Holocaust-related poetry. It's as if there were two different people. At his core, he's a man riddled with worry and concern, and he certainly passed it on to the next generations. He didn't do it deliberately, of course, it's just who he is.

On the other hand, however, he approaches current events with a sharp sense of humor. He has a good grasp on reality and his interpretations of various situations are always a little different. I think that he still lives with a sense that one day the earth will shake violently beneath his feet like it did during the Holocaust, and things will take an immediate turn for the worse. These are feelings he's always had. Perhaps in a way it's what protects him, because if you know that everything can go haywire at any minute, you're always more prepared. But it's also instilled a pervasive anxiety which is unavoidable. I think he's constantly anxious and concerned, and it's no wonder: the experiences he endured as a child would overwhelm anyone. And yet he still takes every opportunity to talk about those experiences. It's his way of dealing with what he went through, and with his current anxiety.

I've read all of Shmuel's books, and he also used to ask my opinion on his unfinished poems. He was delighted when people read his poems, even the unfinished handwritten drafts. Reading the manuscripts or the published works was always a complex emotional challenge. They're a collection of deliberations on survival and destiny, on the trials and tribulations of life, on challenges faced and challenges ahead. It got me thinking what it must be like to be in his shoes, and how much it affected his and his family's lives. Having someone around who is always anxious and gets distressed about every little thing is a difficult situation to be in. Livya, as someone who grew up with her father, has handled it impressively indeed. I've told her many times that if I had grown up with someone like Shmuel, I'm not sure how I would have turned out. I think he's not fully aware of the implications that his constant anxiety has on his family. He's a man of action –saying, doing, telling.

And yet our grandchildren – Guy, Adi, and May – find Shmuel hilariously funny. At every family gathering they ask him questions, eagerly anticipating the answers, enjoying the language, as well as the imagery and the wit. He can be very prickly when asked about various people we know – whether here on the kibbutz or figures from Israeli public life – but it's always tinged with humor.

However, he isn't the most attentive when it comes to others, and he's never really interested in others' stories or experiences. He's focused on his own experiences and above all I believe that he finds it incredibly important to convey his own experiences from the Holocaust and tell the story of the family he lost there. Occasionally he'll snap out of "Holocaust Mode". Usually this will happen when he talks about the Palmach (his old army unit), or places of importance to Israeli and Zionist history, or the Labor party, or the Hapoel Tel Aviv football club, or the kibbutz. These are the main alleyways he uses to escape from the pain.

He's always been very moved when asked to come and tell his story of the Holocaust. He finds it hard to believe that his name is mentioned in various places on the internet. He knows exactly what's been written about him through the years, and collects newspaper clippings and letters. I remember how touched he was by the compliments he received about his poetry from the wife of famous Israeli poet Uri Zvi Greenberg.

I remember when we all went out to celebrate his 80th birthday, he suddenly fell into a deep depression. We were all sitting at the restaurant and we couldn't even toast him. He completely blocked everyone out and refused to continue the festivities. Everyone had come to pay their respects, but he wasn't really there. No one knew exactly why, but eventually we just canceled the rest of the event, finished our food and left. It was as if something had flooded him internally and he didn't want to be part of the occasion any longer. Perhaps the age of eighty invokes questions of life and death; perhaps it was just a bout of uncontrollable anger or other emotions.

I think that's where Shmulik tragically deals with it too much. Without being judgmental, I think his story really dominates his life, possibly without him being aware of it all the time. But that's his way of life, and far be it from me to make any judgments. There are other people who wish nothing more than to forget it all. That too is legitimate, and I have no claims against either way of life.

Over the past few years, his wife Bracha has been ill, and the way he cares for her is admirable. Many people might find it hard to deal with things the way he has for so long, but he does so with great devotion and dedication. I think that telling his story and incessantly writing about the Holocaust – along with his unique sense of humor – is what allows him to survive emotionally. Despite the heaviness of the Holocaust which is an inherent part of Shmuel's personality, he also knows how to enjoy life. Give him a good steak or some sausage and he's content.

**Part Two – My parents and the Holocaust**

My parents were never ones to talk about what happened in the Holocaust. Usually I had to coax them for answers, and a few sentences later it was over. On my mother's side, I always used to ask her sister for more information.

I come from a household where the Holocaust was always in the background. My sister and I were born to Holocaust survivors, and yet I never felt like I grew up as a second-generation survivor. My parents rarely spoke about what had happened, and it was never a central issue at home. My parents wanted to raise us free from fear and anxiety, and I believe they succeeded. My childhood and adolescent years were very pleasant and full of experiences.

When I compare the way Livya grew up to the way I grew up, I really appreciate the way my parents raised me. Just recently my sister and I had a memorial service for our parents. It's been a year since my mother passed and 22 years since my father passed. I spoke about our happy childhood, how our parents encouraged us to be independent and forge our own path. Looking back, and comparing them to Shmuel, I know things could have turned out a lot differently. I think that intuitively – and unwittingly – my parents were great educators.

My father never said anything. Not necessarily out of concern for others; he just internalized it and never spoke of it – probably as a defense mechanism. My mother also lived in denial, and as a second-generation survivor, I've wondered many times what the correct way is of dealing with these things – if such a way exists. My own coping mechanism has evolved over the years. There were times when I was very withdrawn and silent, and there were times when I spoke about it often. I've also wondered what is appropriate to talk about, and what isn't. The quandary intensifies when one thinks of the future generations: What is the appropriate way of passing on the message? How should people approach the education of their children and students?

Both my parents reacted differently to the Holocaust. My father was from Budapest in Hungary. He was imprisoned in Auschwitz in the spring of 1944. After the camp was evacuated in January 1945, he was taken on the death march to the Buchenwald concentration camp in Germany. When the camp was liberated at the end of the war, he left as a "Muselmann" [10]at the age of fifteen. He was transferred by the Red Cross to a sanatorium in Davos, Switzerland, and after he had recuperated, he moved to Israel in the early 1950s.

My father's silence was always deafening. On the very rare occasions he spoke about the Holocaust, it was in a few unsatisfying words. I remember one incident which spoke volumes about his inability to discuss it. I was a teacher at *Einot Yarden* High School, and we had a student exchange with a German school. The German teachers found out that my father had been at the Buchenwald concentration camp. As a nice gesture, they suggested they take the whole group on a tour of the camp, which is near Weimar in East Germany. At the time, the Russians had just returned the entire Nietzsche archives which they had captured from the Germans during

---

10. A German term widely used among concentration camp inmates to refer to prisoners who were near death due to exhaustion, starvation, or hopelessness.

the war. They had been held by the Russians in Leningrad, and after the fall of the USSR and the reunification of Germany, they returned them to the Germans. My German colleagues knew I was writing a thesis on Nietzsche as part of my Master's in Philosophy, and decide to arrange a private tour of the archives, several weeks before it was opened to the public. As soon as I realized we would be going to Buchenwald, I invited my parents for a weekend and implored my father to tell me whatever he could about the camp, as I was going there without much in the way of knowledge. He found it extremely difficult to talk and sat in silence for the entire weekend. Eventually he described the prisoners walking to their forced labor through the main road of the village, and made it clear that the local Germans saw everything. It always bothered him that the Germans used to claim that not everyone knew what was happening. He also told me that many prisoners were shot, and that he himself had been amongst a group of prisoners who were shot, but survived miraculously by playing dead. Three sentences in to his story and he fell silent again, and I couldn't get any further details out of him.

And yet despite everything he had been through, my father was a happy, kindhearted man, very outgoing and diligent, and overall I believe that he enjoyed his life.

My mother, on the other hand, spoke more of the Holocaust. She was born in the Slovak capital of Bratislava. In 1938, when the rumblings of war were becoming more apparent, the family moved to the town of Komárno on the border with Hungary, where they stayed during the war. In the spring of 1944, my mother was sent with her mother and her younger sister Marion to Auschwitz along with the rest of Hungary's Jews. She was about fourteen years old. When they arrived they were separated: their mother was put to death immediately, while my mother and her sister were subjected to forced labor. After a while they were transferred to Plaszow labor camp in Krakow, about 60 miles north of Auschwitz. Later they were sent back to Auschwitz, and afterwards were sent to work at the Luftwaffe parts factory in the town Calw in eastern Germany. Subsequently they were sent on a "death march" – the term for the forced marching of Jewish prisoners by the Germans from concentration camps in eastern Europe back to Germany during the final months of the war, due to the advances of the Russians. Many prisoners died of starvation and cold, and many others were shot. Eventually they reached the town of Buching, where they were liberated. I became aware of this story only when Guy, my eldest son, was thirteen years old. He discovered the story as part of his family roots project; my mother had never mentioned it to me. She used to say, "Even in Auschwitz there were good Germans." It was her way of trying to see the good in every situation. I always found it strange: how could someone who had endured that ordeal talk like that? As a teacher, it took me a long time before I agreed to join the trips to Germany. When I eventually decided to go, I told my mother where we had been, and she said, "Oh, we passed through there on the death march." She had half a smile on her face, too! Subsequently, my memories of these places have somewhat softened due to her own non-tragic outlook. She always lit candles on Holocaust Memorial Day, but she never watched the television programs. She didn't want to see or hear anything to do with the Holocaust. She had a very positive outlook on life, and she wanted her children, the future generation, to forget about the ordeals of the Holocaust.

Her sister, Marion, was with her the whole time during the Holocaust. She too survived, and she spoke about it more often. One of the stories she told was of Dr. Mengele, the murderous doctor who performed brutal experiments on Jewish children at Auschwitz. My mother worked tarring roads outside the camp, and she was constantly getting hurt. One day when her bandages were being changed in the "clinic", Mengele came in suddenly and said, "Get ready, I'll be back soon." Her sister happened to be there, and she understood exactly what was going on. She managed to hide my mother, and when he came back, told him in no uncertain terms that he was wrong – the girl he was looking for wasn't here, and that's how she saved my mother's life.

Right around the time Guy was writing his family roots project, I traveled to Germany in order to organize a joint Israeli-German teachers' seminar. I had a good German friend named Ludwig, who I had earlier met on Kibbutz Shamir. Incidentally, he lived in a town called Ludwigsburg, which houses the "Zentrale Stelle" – the Central Office for the Investigation of National Socialist Crimes. During this trip, I visited the archives along with Ludwig, and I told him that my mother had been one of the prisoners at Calw. Noting his surprise, he told me he owned a book written by historian Josef Seubert about those prisoners. I was equally surprised, as I had had no idea that it was such a well-known story. We went to Ludwig's house and retrieved the book, titled "From Auschwitz to Calw". We immediately called Seubert, and he identified my mother's and her sister's names in the list of prisoners kept at Zentrale Stelle.

Seubert had become aware of the story because he lived near Kusterdingen, a town through which the prisoners passed one night during the death march. They stayed overnight in a barn which had a tree in it, and on this tree they had carved various phrases in Hungarian. Seubert investigated the matter, and discovered that around two-hundred women had left Calw on the death march and had passed through town. On the tree they had carved phrases testifying to the hardships they were being put through. This story was what inspired him to research these women. I asked him where he had obtained the list of names, and he explained that during the 1980s, he managed to track down a Jewish woman from Romania who had been one of those two-hundred women, and she knew all two-hundred names by heart! He could not fathom how on earth she could have remembered all those names decades after the war, and was not certain whether the list was genuine – but he still wrote down all the names and kept the list. When questioned, the woman told him that she knew the names because of all the times they were forced to attend roll call at the camp. It seemed strange to him at the time, and it still seems strange to me now – but I guess there's no other explanation. Eventually, several years later, Seubert discovered the same list with the exact same names, confirming the authenticity of the information.

When I got back to Israel, I brought Seubert's book to my mother. I wasn't sure how she'd react, thinking it might be too overwhelming for her, but when I met her and her sister they were barely moved at all. They also told me another amazing story: When they got to Auschwitz and disembarked from the train, the Nazis began selecting prisoners for extermination or for labor. They didn't know whether to claim that they were younger or older, and people there were giving them conflicting advice. Eventually they decided to say they were older. It was an arbitrary decision which proved to be a life-saving one, because the next day the younger girls were put to death.

Some time later I traveled with my son Guy to Germany, and along with Ludwig and Seubert, traveled the route of the death march from Calw to Buching, which was where my mother was liberated. Ever since I was a boy, the name "Buching" always symbolized freedom for my mother. We drove from Calw through Ulm, Tübingen, and Kusterdingen (the barn where the Jewish women had stayed was no longer there), and ended up in Buching. We stayed the night and the next day we traveled back to Calw. Today the bark shavings from the tree on which the women had carved their messages in Kusterdingen are kept in the Stuttgart Museum of History. At the time, I told the story to a joint Israeli-German delegation of teachers, and was very moved by the occasion. Several years later, just before Guy began his military service, we took another trip with Ludwig, this time in my father's footsteps. We traveled to Davos, Switzerland, where my father had stayed at a sanatorium after the war.

There's one more interesting story about Germany: When I graduated high school, my friend Rani and I went on a cross-European train journey, and I was hesitant about passing through Germany. Rani's family had lived in Germany before the war, and his grandmother had been a doctor. She had saved the life of a German man who was under her care before the Holocaust. His son wanted to meet the grandson of the doctor who had saved his father's life. He felt he owed her a debt of gratitude and wanted to do something in return by hosting her grandson. Rani asked that I join him and stay with the family who lived in Munich. I approached my parents and told them of my predicament. To this day, I remember we sat outside on the porch and had a profoundly serious talk, and my parents' ultimate response was: "Gadi, as always, we trust you completely. We are fine with any decision you make." They were fine with me traveling throughout Europe on trains even before I had reached my 18th birthday, and it didn't seem to bother them at all. Today I wonder if perhaps they were just really good at hiding their concern. Livya's family was the opposite. There was a distinct sense of concern and anxiety that always lingered.

On that trip to Germany I experienced something quite strange. We stayed the night at the family's house in Munich, and in the morning I caught a glimpse of the father of the family while he was brushing his teeth – the same man who had wanted to host Rani out of gratitude for his grandmother. For some reason I still can't explain, I told Rani we had to leave immediately. I assume it reminded me of the story of the Israeli agent who had captured Adolf Eichmann – he famously described how he had observed Eichmann brushing his teeth. And so we left Germany the very same day. The German who had hosted us was no Nazi, but something about the situation made me feel very uncomfortable. Naturally, he was not to blame – he was a very gracious host. It was all in my head of course, but nonetheless, I decided we had to leave. We visited Dachau – the concentration camp situated near Munich – and the memorial for the eleven Israeli athletes murdered during the

1972 Munich Olympic Games, and then left. I told myself then and there that I would never return to Germany. Eventually I did return, but it was only thirteen years later.

**Part Three – Israeli-German Relations**

The issue of my being the son of Holocaust survivors came up quite early in my friendship with my German friend Ludwig. It was perhaps the second time we spoke. He was volunteering at Kibbutz Shamir and we were both working at the swimming pool. We'd come early in the morning, clean the pool, mow the grass, and at some point we'd go to the dining hall, get a basket with some bread and cheese, go back to the swimming pool, eat, and talk. We developed a strong bond quite quickly. During our conversations he mentioned that he came from a Nazi family. I remember once he told me that his father was very ill and that he didn't want to go and visit him. He told me that at the age of ten he had discovered his father's military cap with all the Nazi symbols and insignia, and was devastated when he realized what his family had been mixed up in. He spoke a lot about the forced relocation of his family to the Black Forest area in Bavaria, due to the "de-Nazification" – steps taken by the German government to distance the Nazis and minimize their visibility after the war. His father continued to work as a teacher, but they lived in a remote village in the Black Forest.

Ludwig visited Shamir for the last time about a month before he died. He brought his grandson along with him. We sat on the porch with a few friends, and for the first time, he recounted the entire tale of how he had first come to Shamir until the present day. It was as if he was passing on his legacy to his grandson.

He went back to Germany, and several weeks later he died. The local council sent a small delegation – myself included – to his funeral in Ludwigsburg. In January of 2018, I was also in attendance at the ceremony where Ludwig was posthumously given a lifetime achievement award from the Ludwigsburg local council. We still keep in touch with his widow Marlise, as well as his daughter Christiana and his four grandchildren.

I don't view Israeli-German relations as something that should be normalized. I suppose each person has their own way of looking at it. Personally, I've been to Germany many times as part of educational projects. But I've never been to Germany on vacation. The one time I did something that wasn't work-related in Germany was very recent. We went to Ludwig`s widow Marlise to honor Ludwig's memory one year after his passing. Upon arrival, we learned that she couldn't meet us as planned for the first few days – which meant we now had three or four days with nothing to do. Livya suggested we take a trip to the Black Forest. That was the first time since my trip with Rani after high school that I had taken part in any leisure activities in Germany – and I've been to the country dozens of times. Whenever I go to Germany, I always bring a book on the Holocaust. So each person has their own idea of what relations with Germany should look like.

Educationally speaking, I don't give my students a clear message on how to relate to the Germans. I believe people should act in accordance with their own personal feelings. For example, my father was not entirely at peace with the friendship I shared with Ludwig. He always used to say, "I don't mind having ties with Germans, but I am against any personal friendships."

My mother, on the other hand, was always very friendly with Ludwig. My father had his boundaries and we respected them.

From my vast experience and encounters with Germans, I've learned that they experience the memory of the Holocaust in different ways. During one of my visits to Germany, I became acquainted with a woman named Wendelgard von Staden. She lived in a town called Flehingen, not far from Stuttgart. During the war, when she was about nineteen years old, she discovered that there was a concentration camp in a forest clearing outside the town. After the war, she wrote a fascinating book titled "Darkness over the Valley". During the Holocaust, she had been a member of the League of German Girls, which was affiliated with the Nazi youth movement, the Hitlerjugend. In her book she describes how she joined the movement, and how she had admired Hitler as a leader in her youth. When she grew older she pledged to memorialize the Holocaust in Germany; I came to visit her several times with groups of Israeli and German youths. She is a very pleasant woman, but there were several occasions where the German youths verbally attacked her for her erstwhile support of Hitler. She started crying, and the situation had to be defused quite abruptly. She said that being in the Hitlerjugend was akin to being a part of the Cub Scouts: she hadn't joined because she was an antisemite, but because almost all youths joined. At one point it even became mandatory. German youths today feel a sense of overwhelming guilt. Germans everywhere are forced to grapple with those memories, and not everyone has the mental fortitude or the desire to do so.

On one of the delegations that I was a part of in the early 1990s, I discovered that there was an ongoing trial in Stuttgart against the last Nazi war criminal extradited from Argentina to

Germany, Josef Schwammberger. He had been the commander of the Przemyśl ghetto in Poland, and became famous during the Eichmann trial, when a Jewish dentist who had lived in the ghetto testified that Schwammberger had whipped a young Jewish boy eighty times. When I found out about the trial, I decided to take the group of youths I was with at the time to the courthouse, to witness the trial firsthand. When I enquired about viewing the trial, I was denied permission due to Neo-Nazi protests outside. Uncharacteristically, I stood my ground. I spoke to my friend Ludwig and told him that I had to be allowed inside. He intervened on my behalf and they let us in. The day before, I had a talk with the youths and told them that we would be entering individually or in pairs due to the sensitive nature of the issue at hand, and if anything started happening, they were not to confront anyone. I couldn't sleep that night due to the stress; I feared some of the youths might not handle the situation well. We walked to the court in small groups, apprehensive of a potential encounter with the Neo-Nazis, but we were relieved to learn that there were no protesters there at all. If you ask me, the police probably dispersed them on our account.

The courthouse was small. The Nazi war criminal on trial sat about 30 feet away from us. One of the witnesses was an Israeli Holocaust survivor who had heard there was an Israeli group in the courthouse and chose to testify in Hebrew. Afterwards we got to meet with the prosecutors and the defense lawyers. It was a rare and fascinating experience. When I got back to Israel, I discussed the trial with Shmulik, and marveled at the fact that German citizens were prosecuting their fellow Germans for crimes they had committed on behalf of their country all those years ago. I don't recall exactly what he said, but I remember discussing it with him. He usually wasn't interested in other stories, but this story actually did pique his curiosity. I assume most people who experienced the Holocaust like Shmulik did aren't really emotionally available to hear the plight of others, but this was a rare exception, which is why I remember it so vividly.

I assume that my friendship with Ludwig would have blossomed even if he weren't German, because we shared many interests – human beings, challenges, cultures, philosophy, soccer, jazz music, etc. He wasn't a Nazi; on the contrary – he had been devastated to learn about what they had perpetrated. I'm sure it would have been much more difficult – probably impossible – for me to be friends with someone who had at one time been an active Nazi. It's easier to stimulate a dialogue with the younger German generations, who are burdened with the dark shadows of their past. It creates a sort of shared destiny, and a shared need to face the past.[11]

---

11. The Israeli movie "Walking on Water" (2003), starring Lior Ashkenazi, deals with the issue of Israel-German relations. It tells the story of a Mossad agent sent to assassinate an elderly Nazi officer who has been in hiding for years. The agent, who is the son of Jewish-German Holocaust survivors, befriends the Nazi's grandson in order to gain access to the grandfather and kill him. He also befriends his granddaughter, who lives on a kibbutz in Israel and has cut off ties with her parents because they have helped hide her Nazi grandfather. Eventually she falls in love with the Israeli agent, and they get married. It's a fascinating film which is slightly reminiscent of Gadi's and Ludwig's relationship, insofar as it describes the true friendships which were shared between second- and third-generation Jews and Germans despite the dark shadows of the Holocaust.

**Part Four – Lessons from the Holocaust**

"Lessons from the Holocaust" is a term I've always found interesting. Does such a thing even exist? A moral lesson is, after all, a conclusion, and from a conclusion one attempts to derive values. What values could one derive from the Holocaust? Personally, I think the important questions – which I grapple with often – are the universal human questions. For example, how does one show empathy and understanding toward the suffering of others? How should we instill our own insights from the Holocaust in future generations? How does one generate an awareness for compassion, solidarity, and consideration for others?

To me, one of the most important lessons is that people in positions of power should avoid inflicting suffering on the weak and steer clear of herd mentality. Over the years, I've been influenced by Buddhist values such as bringing good into the world; viewing all living creatures on Earth as equal and valuable; understanding that each person has his or her own calling; and to improve and fix the world. If we act accordingly, we make human tragedies such as the Holocaust less likely. I know it's somewhat naive, but that is the way I think. I'm no politician; I am a man of education, and wherever I can conduct an educational dialogue, I find it important to address not only the Holocaust, but the root causes of all human tragedies around the world.

Educating future generations on the Holocaust also includes delegations such as the ones I participated in over the years in Poland and Germany. I think the question of whether or not to travel to these places is less important than the actual questions one deals with when facing these issues. These are questions one may ask on various levels – whether individually, within a family, or nationally. For example: What drives one to take such a trip, and what does one do on such a trip? What are the definitions of violence and racism? What is human suffering, and how may it be overcome? These are universal, existential, and philosophical questions which relate not only to what happened to the Jewish nation during the Holocaust, but also to the suffering of other nations as well.

I wouldn't be able to separate the Holocaust and the reasons for it from universal life lessons. I believe that it is critical that people are aware that the path from apathy to actively inflicting pain is surprisingly short. How do we avoid that? How do we show understanding and empathy to the plight of others? These are the questions I deal with in my role as an educator, and I raise them whenever possible. For example, I am an avid soccer fan; for several years now I have been volunteering with the New Israel Fund to combat racism and violence at soccer stadiums. I go to games and report acts of violence. I know full well that the scope of my influence is rather meager, but I also know I'm doing my bit to try and make a difference. I believe combating violence should be prioritized in every educational system, procedure, and project. I am a math teacher, and I can guarantee that combating violence is more important than any mathematical concept one could ever hope to learn. Constantly addressing these issues is an educational way of life, and naturally it is not restricted only to the Holocaust.

My sister just returned from Vietnam, and at the latest memorial service for our parents, we had a very thought-provoking discussion. How does the Vietnamese nation, which suffered horrendously during the wars that plagued the country, ostensibly leave everything in the past and decide to look forward? How do they abstain from picking at the wounds of the past? It's an interesting psycho-historical question for a society fighting to escape the clutches of suffering, looking for a way to fuse the past and the future; to live life and constantly think about what messages are being passed on to future generations. I don't think there's one right answer, each individual sees things differently. Personally, I believe people should strive to see what's good and beautiful in the world, and to know that there are forces of evil to be aware of.

**Part Five – Studying and Remembering the Holocaust**

I believe that studies of the Holocaust should be part of an experiential learning process. There's a good example from one of the students at the school I taught at – the Einot Yarden High School. The iconic film "Schindler's List", directed by Steven Spielberg, made a deep impression on her. The film tells the story of Oskar Schindler, a German industrialist who saved many of his Jewish workers at the Plaszow labor camp near Krakow in Poland. She began to search for the woman that Amon Göth, the commander of the camp, had made his mistress. She discovered she was still alive and living in Holon, Israel. She contacted her and the whole class went to meet her in Tel Aviv. She came along with her son to talk to us, and it was an incredible experience.

I also led a project with one of my classes on the legal aspects of the Holocaust. At the time, during the late 1980s, the trial of Ivan Demjanjuk was ongoing in Israel. Demjanjuk was a Ukrainian who served in the SS and was charged with abusing Jewish prisoners at the Treblinka extermination camp in Poland.

I thought we could use the opportunity to grapple with several Holocaust issues by way of legal quandaries. I split the students into small groups, and each group picked a theme for a trial and presented it to the other students. Each group also wrote down three or four legal questions they had, such as "Why is there a statute of limitations on Nazi war crimes?" We compiled a list of questions and I called Judge Chaim Cohen, who was at the time the Attorney General of Israel, and asked whether we could come to his home in Jerusalem and raise the questions for discussion with him. To my delight, he agreed. We traveled to his home on Tchernichovsky St. in Jerusalem, and started peppering him with questions. At some point he said he needed help, so he called Judge Ruth Gavison to assist him. We sat with them for hours, and they answered all the questions that were bothering us. No doubt it was a fascinating and unforgettable evening!

Whenever these issues come up during Holocaust seminars, I find myself thinking how lucky I am not to have been born into a reality like that. What would I do? Would I initiate an uprising and leave my family for dead? I think that the way to do it is to address the issues of the Holocaust without losing sight of living your own life. Finding a way to memorialize the past and to move on at the same time is not an easy task. Some people would say we're better off forgetting.

I remember a long discussion I had with Orna Ben-Dor Niv, who directed the film "Because of That War" about Israeli musical artist Yehuda Poliker, who is the son of Jewish-Greek Holocaust survivors. I remember she said something that resonated with me, about how she had become so deeply embroiled in the Holocaust and couldn't stop thinking about it, so she decided to stop making movies about the Holocaust. She felt it was just too much. And yet a year later, I saw she had directed a new film about the Holocaust. I called her up and asked her about it and she said, "Indeed, I couldn't help myself. I'm addicted." I find it important to address the Holocaust, because I feel that if I don't, I might distance myself too much. But I do try and maintain boundaries – I want to avoid dealing with it obsessively, and I attempt to make it a part of my life that's always there, but doesn't change or overwhelm my own life.

As an educator, I find it important to think about the interactions derived from your own personal experiences, and searching for answers to an issue as complex as the Holocaust requires a delicate balance.

There is definitely a difference between first-, second- and third-generation survivors, certainly as it pertains to the experience itself and the memory of it. I remember a social worker who wrote a research paper on second-generation survivors once said, "Each family has one memorial candle," meaning there's usually only one person in each family who deals with the memory of the Holocaust. My sister, for example, never really addressed it much. And I bear no grudges towards her or anyone else. Each individual has his or her own way of dealing with things, and if someone were to come to me and tell me that the memory of the Holocaust is disrupting his life, I'd tell him to stop thinking about it all the time. Someone else might tell him to keep at it despite the pain. As with so many things, it's highly personal. I find it something that is almost impossible to get away from. I have always felt that the memory of the Holocaust is something important that I feel almost compelled to address in my everyday life.

# CHAPTER 14:
# THE STORY OF GUY LAHAV

**"Grandpa is a mixture of pain and humor"**
Guy is the eldest grandchild of Shmuel and Bracha Sucha, and the eldest son of Livya and Gadi Lahav. He is married to Aviva. Their children are Yahli-Yehudit and Ziv.

*This chapter includes parts of conversations between Guy and the author.
**Questions and remarks by the author are in bold typeface.**

There are a few things I'd like to talk about. Regarding kindergarten, I don't really recall exact stories, but rather the experience itself. On Holocaust Memorial Day, my grandfather would come to the kindergarten and all the children would sit in a circle while he told us about the Holocaust. And then the other end of the scale was him coming on Hanukkah and putting on a show for us called "Rabbi Kalman and Hannah Zelda". Those were the two sides of the person that is my grandfather: profound pain and unique humor. Those are the things that I grew up knowing. Grandpa is a mixture of pain and humor. Those experiences from kindergarten made such an impression on me that years later, when I attended a preparatory military academy before being drafted into the IDF, I decided to bring my friends from the academy to Kibbutz Shamir to learn about the Holocaust. We met with Grandpa and with the late Moshe Kagan, another kibbutz member and Holocaust survivor, and listened to their stories.

**Moshe Kagan has a somewhat different story. He was from the town of Kremenets', about 100 miles from Bereźne, where your grandfather was born. Kagan was older than your grandfather, he was about twenty years old when the war started in 1941. His family was murdered by the Germans but he managed to flee east, deep into Soviet territory, and he was drafted into the Russian Red Army. He was part of a division of Polish soldiers who had managed to escape to the USSR following the German occupation. He served as an officer and fought the Germans in multiple battles, including the Battle for Berlin.**

As a child, it felt good that Grandpa came to tell us his stories. Anytime he came I felt like I had an opportunity to show off my family to the other kids and I felt very proud! It was a positive experience for me, and I even anticipated it somewhat… I don't recall it being traumatic at all. I think he always knew how to adapt his stories based on his audience. He never said anything horrific. I mostly remember the stories about the forest: looking for food, climbing trees, gathering crows' eggs, picking blueberries, collecting seeds, foraging for mushrooms, learning which ones were poisonous and which were edible.

When I grew older and heard his stories again, there were other details which I assume he mentioned for the first time since he thought I was now ready to hear them: his first night in the forest, walking for hours until his feet hurt, darkness falling over the forest, and not knowing where to stop and rest. Eventually he entered a small, empty animal's lair, and tried to sleep. But despite being exhausted, the loneliness and fear of the unknown prevented him from falling asleep.

I remember asking him when he began writing. He said it was in the DP camp in Germany. There was one boy who was harassing my grandfather in some way, and his method of dealing with it was to write. He suddenly realized that he was a very good writer, and since then has employed his writing in various scenarios: in the youth movement, as a journalist, and later on also in his Holocaust poetry and stories.

My grandparents made three trips to Ukraine, and I joined them on the second one, along with my mother Livya. That was in 2005, after I had graduated high school and before I was drafted into the army. It was actually a journey in my grandfather's footsteps. I have two very powerful memories: One was the speech he wrote and read aloud on behalf of the group at the unveiling of the Bereźne memorial for the town's Jews who had been murdered in the Holocaust. The other was while we were on the bus in the forests near Bereźne. In the middle of the road he yelled to the bus driver, "Stop!" and asked to get off the bus. He disembarked, and walked into the forest. Some of us followed him out of curiosity. He was walking amongst the trees, examining the blueberries, picking the good ones and eating them. It was almost nostalgic for him. I remember the glint in his eyes, he was like a child who had returned home.

My grandfather loves to eat. I don't know many people who enjoy food quite like he does, even if he does have something of an odd taste. He has a habit of eating something sour at the end of every meal. When we were in Ukraine, he wasn't interested in any of the restaurants. He preferred to go into a local grocery store, buy some bread and sardines and pickles, and sit and eat on the steps outside the store. It must have had something to do with the simplicity or the memory of certain foods. He enjoyed it immensely.

If I may circle back to the meeting we had with him at the pre-military academy, there's something I must note about his unique way of telling his Holocaust stories. I've been present at multiple talks with Holocaust survivors, and it's always a heavy, grave topic. But with my grandfather it's different. We were all sitting there with him at the kibbutz clubhouse, and people were laughing out loud. It wasn't awkward laughter either; it was genuine laughter evoked by his unique sense of humor. He is a man of imagery. He wanted to illustrate to us how dirty he was, and he told us that it was so bad that if he had taken off his clothes and laid them on the floor, they would have started moving on their own because of all the lice. That got a good laugh out of the boys.

**I've also noticed that his stories are tinged with a smile. That's a big part of his charm. I call it "The Holocaust with a Smile". This is not to mean that it brings him joy, of course. It's just a form of storytelling that makes it easier for the listener to stay attentive, and to identify with the storyteller.**

People have always felt at ease around my grandfather. There was never any tension in the air, and people never left in tears. Despite the sheer horror of the events, people laugh because of the way he tells his stories. And they are endless! He definitely has a knack for seeing the humorous side of things. And he's got a sly side to him as well. He once told me that before they boarded the ship to come to Palestine, he had to be weighed to make sure he met the health criteria. He was underweight, so the next time he put rocks in his pockets to tip the scales in his favor.

Another very prominent feature of my grandfather's is the very strong desire not to die. He exercises a lot, and tries to stay as young as possible. When we were children, he always used to tell us that he would never die.

Another thing he loved to do when we were children was to take photographs of us. He was an avid amateur photographer. After all, he has the soul of an artist; you can tell from his photographs, or from his poetry which he often improvises. We recently had a birthday party for his great-granddaughter, my own daughter Yahli, and he improvised a beautiful poem for her. I wish I had written it down at the time. He also wrote a poem for my Bar Mitzvah. I've never known how long he actually spends on a poem, but from what I've heard, it can be a matter of a few effortless seconds. He's written many books, mostly of poems. I've read his novel "A Fragment from the Planet of Ashes", and many of his poems. I find them to be more depressing than the actual stories.

My grandfather has told me many stories about the Holocaust, and once I even taped him. I had many questions, and I think the whole recording lasted an hour. I was there with my ex-girlfriend, during my military service. It was probably in 2006 or 2007. The reason for my inquisitiveness at the time was because after reading his autobiographical novel, "A Fragment from the Planet of the Ashes", I found it hard to discern the difference between fiction and reality. I also wanted to hear the real story in full. There's a difference between the way he writes and the way he talks, and I thought of it as a good opportunity to record his spoken thoughts rather than his written ones.

When I was working on my Family Roots project for my Bar Mitzvah, I spoke with my mother Livya about her experiences as the daughter of Holocaust survivors. As a third-generation survivor, I was interested in hearing the experiences of a second-generation survivor: kibbutz life, how she was educated, and various things she thought of as being caused by the scars of the Holocaust. She remembered that when she was a teenager, my grandfather was always worried about her traveling on her own, fearing she might be attacked. He was very anxious, and she became that way too as a result.

I don't think I inherited any of the scars of the Holocaust. The way my mother passed them on to me was more filtered, and it never affected my character. I was aware of how everything affected her, but I was more of an observer, and never really experienced things the way she had. I certainly found it interesting, and on occasion, it helped me understand the way she and my grandfather behaved.

The trip to Ukraine was certainly a rare opportunity for me to see the two of them together for a sustained period of time. It wasn't that I never believed the stories she used to tell me, but being there with the two of them really gave me a perspective of the intensity of the experiences themselves. Despite the heavy burden of the Holocaust hanging over the trip by its very nature, it was ultimately a positive experience.

Fortunately, my mother videotaped much of the trip to Ukraine. I believe that documentation is very important. It's unfortunate that my grandfather never adapted to technological advances, because he may well have written even more than he did. He still uses a pencil and never learned to use a computer. I tried to teach him several times to type on a computer, but I guess it was just too late.

**I think that to him, writing is a method both for conveying memories and for emotional release. It's important to note that those murdered during the Holocaust requested two things: remembrance and vengeance. It's a theme that arises in almost every testimony, and the survivors often view themselves as those responsible for carrying out those wishes. Those experiences never totally become a thing of the past – survivors relive them again and again. Your grandfather's themes are mostly related to his sister, his parents, and his uncle. He actually relives those experiences every day. We know this to be one of the great difficulties of living as a Holocaust survivor.**

Did you ask him if he felt the need for vengeance?

**I asked him, and he told me that he did. He never actually killed anyone personally, but he did approach the NKVD (the Soviet secret police) and pointed out those people he wanted to exact revenge upon. Eventually they were executed or sent to Siberian labor camps, which usually meant a death sentence carried out more slowly. His need for vengeance was strong, but it came only after liberation, because during the**

war he was occupied with day-to-day survival. After the war, vengeance was very much on the minds of the survivors and their families. But you should know that Israel as a state was rarely ever in the revenge business. There are several books on the topic, notably "The Avengers" written by Michael Bar Zohar (Bar Zohar, 1967). Abba Kovner, a Lithuanian Holocaust survivor who later became a well-known author, was the ideological leader of "The Avengers", a group of survivors formed with the aim of exacting revenge upon the Nazis. Their main plot was a failed attempt to poison the water supplies of several cities in Germany, in a bid to kill as many Germans as possible. There was also another group, comprised of Jewish fighters from Palestine who fought within the Jewish Brigade, a military formation of the British Army which had fought against the Germans in Italy. After the war, between 1945 and 1947, they were active in Germany, Austria, and Italy, killing anywhere from several dozen to several hundred Nazi SS members. However, this was a private endeavor not endorsed by the Jewish authorities in Palestine. Even after the War of Independence, the State of Israel almost never engaged in Nazi hunting. It wasn't high on the priority list, as the fledgling state was too occupied with its survival against the Arab threat. The 1960 capture of Adolf Eichmann, the main administrator of the mass extermination of European Jews, was a rare event. The initiative wasn't originally an Israeli one, but was initially led by a group of German and Argentinian Jews who compiled information on Eichmann and discovered his place of hiding in Buenos Aires. The main planner was Dr. Fritz Bauer, a German-Jewish jurist who was the attorney-general of Hessen. He and others approached then-prime minister David Ben Gurion and pressured him to capture Eichmann, to which he eventually agreed. There was another well-known assassination carried out by the Mossad (the Israeli secret intelligence service) in Uruguay in 1965. This was the killing of Herberts Cukurs, a Latvian SS collaborator nicknamed "The Butcher of Riga" who was responsible for the murder of many Latvian Jews. Other than these, I am not aware of any attempts by the State of Israel to apprehend or assassinate Nazi war criminals, but the desire for revenge has always been very powerful.

That is definitely something that has been passed down from generation to generation. I remember as children, we used to fantasize about what we would do to Mengele…

Mengele was the chief doctor of the Auschwitz-Birkenau concentration camp, who carried out a series of horrific experiments on women and children. After the war he hid in South America. The Mossad tailed him for a while, but the operation was aborted due to the fact that apprehending or assassinating him was not high on the priority list of 1960s Israel.

Today there is almost no one left to take revenge upon. However, the remembrance part of the victims' dying wishes is certainly possible. Remembrance is always relevant, and all generations can do their part by memorializing the Holocaust and passing on the story to the next generation. This is of the utmost importance, and the survivors make this known in no uncertain terms. This is also the reason that your

**grandfather so badly wants his children, grandchildren, and even great-grandchildren to hear the stories and accompany him to Bereźne – the intergenerational storytelling aspect is incredibly important.**

The third-generation perception is definitely unique. Once, on a family trip to Germany in the footsteps of my paternal grandmother's Holocaust experience, I helped an elderly woman up the steps of the Berlin Metro. As I was helping her up, I began to wonder whether the woman I was assisting had been a Nazi during the war, and whether she had participated in the murder of Jews.

**Statistically speaking, there is a chance that she was a Nazi, because most Germans were at the time Nazis due to the fact they identified with Nazi Germany. Have you ever asked your grandfather if he would have a problem with one of his grandchildren marrying a German?**

I have, and he said he wouldn't care. He has no issues with younger Germans, and I'm not surprised. He's never had much of an anti-German sentiment. Perhaps it's because his own Holocaust experience was perpetrated by the Ukrainians.

**I think so too. Those he attempted to take revenge upon after the war were all Ukrainians who had directly harmed him or his family. However, many Israelis still have great difficulty accepting Germany and the German people. My late grandfather, whose family was almost entirely wiped out in the Holocaust, wanted nothing to do with Germany until the day he died. Your grandfather had a different experience.**

My grandfather told me that he had a grandfather who traveled to Montreal, Canada, before the war, with the hope of relocating his family there. However, all contact with him was lost. I've always thought that one day we may find him. We've recently reconnected with part of my father's family from Hungary. One of his uncles is a survivor of Auschwitz, who married a Christian woman after the war and lived with her for years in Budapest. After many years of no contact with them, we finally reconnected.

**The theme of Eastern-European Jewish males immigrating to the US or Canada before the war, with the express intention of being naturalized and relocating their families, is well known. There have been many cases of such men never actually relocating their families, rather severing all ties with them and creating new lives with new families.**
**I would now like to ask you, what do you think are the lessons that should be learned from the Holocaust?**

I think about the Holocaust quite a bit, and I think the most important personal lesson one can learn from it is just to "be a human being". It's how I've been raised ever since I was a small child. My interpretation of it is to be empathetic towards others, not to do unto others what I wouldn't want done to myself, and to take responsibility for social change where I deem it to be necessary.

On the national scale, the Holocaust serves as a painful reminder that the Jewish nation requires its own sovereign state which is capable of defending its citizens and all Jews wherever they may be.

DR. SHAY EFRAT | 207

And universally, the Holocaust serves as a reminder of the dark side of humans, of the potential for evil that exists everywhere.

We must always acknowledge, remember, teach, and educate about the Holocaust so that it is never repeated.

And in closing, I would like to say that we have all benefited from you undertaking this project!

# AFTERWORD

It has been about forty-eight years since I first met Shmuel Sucha at the petting zoo in Kibbutz Shamir. I was eight years old, and he was forty-three. I am now in my fifties and he is in his nineties; yet he still has energy and strength within him. On my morning and evening walks with my dog Snoopy, I often run into Shmuel on his daily bottle-collecting missions. I always know it's him when I see the untied flaps of his mobility scooter swaying in the evening breeze. "It's a hobby," he explains when we meet by the garbage disposal unit by my house, where he stops to collect his bottles. "I do this every day, in any weather." I tell him that it reminds me of what he did during the Holocaust – journeying out every day in search of food.

Shmuel always takes interest in how the book is coming along, and once he gets a progress report from me, he says, "Good, so there's something to live for." We exchange a few words and say goodbye. We have become much closer during these past few years in which I have interviewed him extensively. Ultimately, despite the age gap, we share a common destiny and feel close to each other. Shmuel is a man who has been through just about everything in life, and in many ways his own story is the story of a generation – the generation that survived the Holocaust and founded the State of Israel. As a third-generation survivor, I view myself as responsible for carrying the torch of the memory of the Holocaust. Shmuel Sucha did his part to pass on the memories and stories of the Holocaust, striving to do so ever since he left the Ukrainian forest at the age of thirteen. He lived to tell the tale, and I am here to pass it on.

# REFERENCES

Bejgiel, G. (1954). *My Town Bereźne. A Collection of Memories of Bereźne Survivors in Israel and Abroad*. Privately Published.

Brayer, S. (1996). Rebellion in Kostopol. *We Would Not Go Like Lambs to the Slaughter*. Yaron Golan Publishing.

Finkelstein, G. (1994). *Genya*. Miskal Publishing.

Spector, S. (1990). Volhynia and Polesia. *The Encyclopedia of Jewish Communities Before and During the Holocaust*. (Volume Five). Yad Vashem.

Digital archive of Yad Vashem. (2017). *Testimonies for the USC Shoah Foundation. Videotaped Testimonies of Bereźne Survivors*. Yad Vashem.

Made in United States
Orlando, FL
05 April 2023

31760008R00129